Tales from a ⌇⌇⌇⌇⌇⌇⌇

Tales from a Travelling Mum

Navigating Europe with a Babe-in-Arms

Alice Griffin

First Published in 2009 by Pink Moon Publishing
(www.pinkmoonpublishing.com)

Typeset in Book Antiqua

**The name of the village Alice lived in during her time
in Almería is fictional to ensure the privacy of her
friends living there.**

Cover Illustration © by Joana Soares
www.xengodelengotengo.blogspot.com

*For Mum & Dad who continue
to nurture my adventurous spirit.*

*For Scott, Isabella & Milla, a memento,
written with much love.*

Praise

"Alice has written a number of features for the Babyworld travel section. Alice presents a real hands-on mum approach and writes informative and amusing features of what it is really like travelling with a baby. Her advice and top tips will be of great use to other parents looking to embark on a travelling adventure."

Debbie Bird, Editor,
www.babyworld.co.uk

"This inspiring and evocative book just goes to show that with a spirit of adventure, a touch of humour and more than a little bit of bloody-mindedness, travelling with a baby can be a rich and exciting experience. If this book doesn't give you itchy feet and the confidence to travel with your brood then nothing will!"

Wendy Shand, Mum of three,
Founder, www.totstotravel.co.uk

"This book offers all the encouragement you need to take the exciting leap into travelling with your children. In addition, the two chapters on Spain offer a beautiful insight into life in this wonderful country."

Jan Cooney, Editor,
Spanish Sun Newspaper
www.sunnews.es

"Alice really reaches out to fellow mums with this book. Her mix of humour and honesty gives a realistic view of what it's like travelling with a baby, yet her clear enjoyment of the challenges ensures that you are left feeling that you want to do it too!"

Aliya Daya, Editor, Mumsense Magazine,
www.mumsensemagazine.com

"If you've ever thought — or been told — that travelling with a baby is impossible, think again. Alice speaks from experience when she says that travel with your child is not only possible, but intensely rewarding. Her story is an inspiring and encouraging ready for any parents with a desire to see the world and share it with their child."

Eric Daams, Dad of one, Editor,
www.travelblogs.com and www.travellerspoint.com

"If you want inspiration AND practical tips on travelling with a baby or toddler, read this book! Whether you are simply wanting some inspiration in your armchair or are about to set off on your own travels, this is a lovely read."

Antonia Chitty,
www.familyfriendlyworking.co.uk

"Alice has been writing a family travel column for Twittermoms over the last year and has built up quite a following with her engaging stories about travelling with a baby. I am so excited to finally see all her tips and beautiful tales together in one place."

Megan Calhoun, Founder,
www.twittermoms.com

"It's brilliant to see a popular mummy blogger get published! Alice's book is filled with beautiful, honest and inspirational writing – her blog readers will not be disappointed."

Susanna Scott, Founder,
www.britishmummybloggers.co.uk
and Top 10 British Mummy Blogger,
www.amodernmother.com

"Wonderfully evocative and informative, Tales from a Travelling Mum is a must-read for all parents keen to satisfy their wanderlust with children in tow."

Liz Jarvis, Editor, LivingwithKids

Acknowledgements

I want to start this book by saying a big thank you to all those who read my blog because undoubtedly, this outlet for my writing has played a huge part in my becoming published. There are some who have been with me right from the beginning when, on a rainy day in my garden office I made the choice to chart our move towards life on the road. There are many who have dipped in and out of our story along the way and there are new people stopping by daily. I wish I could write some names but I realise that if I did I would end up spending sleepless nights fretting over those I had accidentally forgotten. So, I will simply say a thank you to you all. As someone who previously scoffed at social media and blogs, I am so glad that I eventually came round. Without these media I am positive that I would not have gained the confidence to make the move from scribbling my thoughts and observations privately in notebooks to approaching editors for work. And, well, if I hadn't made that leap then I probably wouldn't be writing this now. So, to all my Facebook, Twitter and comment box friends – a sincere thank you for enjoying my writing and making me feel I have something worth sharing.

I would also like to thank Dogs Today magazine who first gave me the chance to write professionally about our travels, Babyworld for starting me on the journey of writing about travels with my daughter and to my publisher, Debbie Jenkins, for sowing the book seed and making me consider that I might have a longer story to tell … and of course for being so approachable and patient with my many queries. I will bake you a cake one of these days! In addition, many thanks go to Megan Calhoun at Twittermoms, Jan Cooney at The Spanish Sun newspaper and Aliya Daya at Mumsense magazine, for running my regular columns.

Special thanks must go to travelling mums Tanya, Tina, Gail and Linda, who make up chapter 12. I am so glad that you agreed to be involved in this project because I really feel that you all bring something special to this book. Thanks also to all those who agreed to receive an advance copy and liked it enough to give a testimonial. In particular I would like to thank Laura Tenison at JoJo Maman Bebe for enjoying my little book enough to write the foreword – it is wonderful to have such an inspirational business woman and fellow traveller on board. I must also give a big thank you to my editor Sylvia Howe for her eagle eyes and also for helping me see my book as a reader.

I would also like to express my heartfelt gratitude to artist, Joana Soares, who very kindly agreed to create the painting for my book cover. I met Joana online through the blogging sphere and was lucky enough to meet her and her wonderful family in the flesh during recent travels in Portugal. Joana, not only have you helped me on my journey to find where home is, but you have done a beautiful job of putting all of my words into one delicious painting. You are truly talented!

Lastly, and most importantly, thank you to all my real life friends and family for listening to me rant, ramble and bore you with numerous hare-brained ideas about what I want to do in my life. You know who you are and I hope you know how much it means to me that you accept my craziness and love me just the same.

Foreword

The year I became pregnant with my first child, JoJo had been trading for four years and was expanding rapidly. I was a workaholic, often spending 18 hours a day in our tiny office; handling most areas of the business from designing the maternity and baby collections, to taking customer service calls and visiting factories across the world. I loved my job and was passionate about the brand but I was thrilled to be pregnant with my own child at last.

My euphoria was short lived as time and time again I was told; "You'll lose your ambition now you have a baby" or "I suppose you will be looking to sell now" or even "You think it will be easy, but after the birth you just won't cope".

Whilst I was well aware that having a baby was a huge commitment I had no desire or financial option but to keep running JoJo. I had a team of employees who relied on me and we could not afford a maternity cover MD. But I was determined to bring up my children myself with just a little help and like Alice and her travelling – *I would have children and I would keep running my business!*

As a result Ben and later on Toby travelled with me to factories and were brought along as models on our photo shoots. I remember pacing up and down a hotel room in Greece at 3am trying to get them back to sleep. Toby had woken up crying for his feed which woke Ben who also started howling. With one on my shoulder and the other on my hip, I spent two hours trying to soothe them. The next day I managed a photo shoot with 30 other children. I was totally exhausted but would go through that night many times in order not to be parted from my boys.

As Alice and all mothers know, it is not easy trying to juggle young babies with an active life and at times you may be near breaking point. The reality is that we willingly give up elements of our pre-baby life because children add so much more. The moments that Alice describes so sweetly in her book; when the baby is content and she and her partner are relaxed in the knowledge that they made the right decisions, sum it all up. This book is refreshing and makes an encouraging read for concerned pregnant women expecting their first child and all new mums and dads. You will laugh and empathize with the very real situations the family experience on their journey through life with a baby.

Whether you are a working mother or not we must all remember happy parents make happy babies. Juggling a busy life and a new baby can be challenging but the rewards far outweigh the effort.

Laura Tenison MBE
Founder & Managing Director
JoJo Maman Bébé

Introduction

Before I start, I guess it is important for me to tell you a little about myself and how I ended up writing about travels with my daughter, Isabella, my husband, Scott and our pooch, Milla. It's a fairly simple tale about a girl with a spirit for adventure.

Travel has always played a part – consciously or unconsciously - in most of my decisions. It has been an escape to gather my thoughts, the focus of a new work direction or more often than not, simply because I just can't help it. As a child, I would dream of far-off lands, and wrote stories of amazing places I had visited in my head. Short journeys became fun-filled adventures – even something as prosaic as packing lunch for the day and heading off to climb trees with my friend - to the next estate - became a long and treacherous expedition. My imagination could not be reined in!

At 12 I went on holiday with my parents to Austria. I convinced them that instead of going on the organised tour, I was more than capable of looking after myself and opted to saunter around cobbled alleyways and sit with locals in the village church pondering, ever so romantically, my quest for a life less ordinary. I guess I've always been a bit of an explorer.

And then at 23 life truly started and my dreams of travel to far off places finally became reality when I had the opportunity to spend six months in Japan. The new sights and smells played havoc with my emotions.

Ramen noodles cooked ferociously for impatient businessmen, backstreet restaurants where grease and smoke clung to the air with a heavy sweetness, twilight strolls through Kyoto where geisha girls moved hurriedly along cobbled alleyways, heads bowed. My hunger to see new corners of the world became unstoppable. In the 10 years since then it has not waned.

There have been dusty train trips across the South of France in packed carriages rattling along against a backdrop of motionless blue sea, where I sweated freely in the hot and heavy air. Sodden road trips through the mountains of Northern Spain with hastily-created food served to me on a chipped plate by a proprietor who sat and smoked steadily through the dusky evening, watching silently to see if I liked it. Island hopping in Greece where olive groves and fishing ports found their way into my mind's eye from the back of a moped as the sweet smell of pine seeped into my nostrils. And then, after much hounding of travel publications about my being perfect for the position of writer, assistant or tea-maker extraordinaire – just to get my foot into a world where travel could become my work – I got lucky.

Recruited by a UK-based travel guide as a researcher I couldn't have been happier. Travelling the world as a single woman I felt a thrill like never before, developed a 'there is always a way to get through every eventuality' attitude and embraced each challenge with gusto. The Canadian Rockies in the depths of winter were the backdrop to a breathtaking albeit scary road-trip where I had my first true experience of what it feels like to be alone with only fearsome elk for company. I thrived in the madness of Thailand, hailing rural taxis (strange converted vans to you and me) like a local and clinging on for dear life as a makeshift bike with a metal contraption attached snaked its way off-road with me and another woman, holding tight to her weekly shopping, on board. And once again I knew that exploration would always be part of me.

Then I fell in love. In a heart-stopping – I could tame the traveller in me for this one – way. Soon after there was talk of children and in the nine months spent nurturing our unborn child, together we toyed with the idea that we might put behind us the spontaneous and independent days of travel we had both enjoyed. I'm pleased to say that this notion was short-lived when, over tapas in a local restaurant, me heavily pregnant, we quickly decided that although we were soon to be a family, there was no need to be pushed and prodded into the waiting transfers of all-inclusive holidays. Instead we were going to pass our individual spirit for adventure and freedom onto our unborn child.

Isabella may as well have had her passport photos taken by the photographer who sauntered around the maternity ward, as it wasn't long after that that her ticket to travel arrived. In the two years since then, we have travelled to Norway, France, Greece and Spain, by car, train, bus, plane, taxi and boat, on long and short journeys. These are what I will be sharing with you here. Why, you may ask? Well, from the moment I started to travel with my daughter I wondered what all the fuss was about. I realised quickly that with a bit of planning and a relaxed attitude you can get as much, if not more, joy from travelling with your child. This revelation surprised me and thus my hope for this book, as well as endeavouring to take you to wonderful destinations in your mind, is to hopefully inspire you, reader, to embark on your own family travels. If after reading my words you reach for a backpack, buy a one-way ticket to Greece and are spotted expertly eating stuffed vine leaves in a taverna with one hand, rocking your baby to sleep with the other, I would be a very happy teller of tales. Essentially I want to show that travels with a baby in your backpack can be exciting and fun. I would however like to add that my story is based on travelling with one child; if you have more it might be trickier, but this is a start!

I hope that you will enjoy reading our story as much as we enjoyed creating it.

Alice Griffin
www.alicegriffin.co.uk

Contents

Praise
Acknowledgements
Foreword by Laura Tenison MBE
Introduction
Contents

Are You Mad?...1
Who Says You Can't Travel With A Baby?.......................1
Why Choose Independent Travel With A Baby? 3
Seeing The World With Fresh Eyes 5
Maintaining Your Adventurous Spirit.............................7
What Kind of Trip? 8
The Benefits of Pre-School Travel...............................10
Worldly Intentions 12
Bonjour France! On The Road at Eight Weeks.........13
Planning The First Road Trip 13
The Sea From A Car Seat...16
Sleeping, Changing, Feeding... In A Car 17
Bed & Breakfast... Baby Style 20
My New Accessory..22
Stuck In Paris Traffic On The Road Home.....................23
Mama Mia! Flying Greek at Three Months...............27
The Skies Are Blue...27
Taxi, Boat, Bus... Bring it on! 29
Little Swimmer...34
Gimme, Gimme ,Gimme Milk After Midnight.................37
Ahoy Captain! Magical Norway at Eight Months 41
Beautiful Bergen..41
Café Culture & The View From The Top 43
Out On The Town & In Search of Cheap Wine 46
Out On The Boat..48

Greece By All Means... A Whistlestop Tour **51**
Planning The Long Journey.. *51*
Away We Go... How To Enjoy Wine On A Plane *53*
Making Connections *55*
Strangers On The Boat To Skopelos.................................... *59*
Easter With Friends... *60*
Athens On A Budget... *64*
Open-Ended Family Travel... **69**
Taking To The Roads of Europe *69*
Life As We Know It Is Over *72*
Our New Camper Home *74*
Everyday Life In A Small Space.. *77*
Preparing For Our Departure *79*
Let The Road Trip Begin **83**
Call Of The Road... *83*
First Stop Champagne *84*
Getting Into Routine On Site.. *87*
In-Car Entertainment... *89*
Looking For The Sunshine... *91*
The South of France **95**
The Kindness Of Strangers *95*
City Camping.. *98*
Stranded In The South of France....................................... *101*
Rainy Days & Playtime... *103*
The Family Make Hay... *106*
Viva España! **111**
Fiestas, Siestas & Sangria.. *111*
Friends In The Olive Groves *113*
To The Mountains... *116*
Making Friends... *119*
Captured by Almendra **123**
We Just Couldn't Leave *123*
Winter In The Mountains.. *126*
Olive Picking In Extremadura *129*
Plans To Move On *132*
Sad Farewells *135*

Where To Next?..**137**

Inspirational Stories from Other Travelling Mums **139**

Introduction by Alice *139*

Tanya Whitehead *140*

Tina Norman *145*

Gail Mowat *147*

Linda Jones *153*

Tips and Advice

B&Bs and Self Catering

Bathing

Beach

Camping & Caravanning

Car

Changing & Toileting

City Breaks

Confidence & Consideration

Feeding

Hotels

Out On The Town

Packing

Tips For Peace And Quiet

Plane

Preparation & Planning

Sleeping

Travelling (while you are there)

Useful Items

Walking

Working Holidays

Useful Websites

Bibliography

About Alice Griffin

CHAPTER ONE

Are You Mad?

Who Says You Can't Travel With A Baby?

What is it about having a bump that makes complete strangers feel they have the right to reach out, touch your growing baby and accompany that invasion with advice that they believe will prepare you for impending motherhood? Of course, it didn't help that at the time of my pregnancy I worked in a shop where a constant stream of women wandered daily through the door, all with a deep and profound knowledge of life after giving birth and all eager to share this knowledge with me. Like bees to honey I found myself overwhelmed by the swarm, and for a while life began to revolve around those sweet moments, usually in the storeroom, where I could silently come up for air. Granted, some of the advice was great, but the bits I didn't like were the ominous predictions that life as I knew it would change dramatically.

"And how might it change?" I asked one such customer, sarcastically. She replied in an energetic, "I won't say I told you so… but I did," tone.

"Oh! Don't start me off, love! Once you have that child you can forget about life as you know it. Oh yes, and that travelling lark you're so fond of – ooo, that will be out of the window straight away!" I smiled and shrugged, but walking home I started to wonder whether it was really

1

true. Would my beloved independent travelling - which had given me so much pleasure - really have to go?

Over the years it had saved me in times of distress, energised me in periods of discouragement and fed my hunger for spontaneity quite wonderfully. Surely it would not have to end when I became a mother. I wanted to retain a bit of me – Alice, the individual. The girl in flip-flops walking off, plumes of dust in her wake, along an unbeaten rugged track looking for somewhere to sit and ponder whatever new country I might be exploring. A place where ice-cold local beer would be served up accompanied by the cadence of an unknown language and a face that would be puzzled by me, the tourist. Thoughts of me relinquishing my spirit for delving into these quiet corners of the world to opt for the all-inclusive, minimal hassle, maximum relaxation option - with egg and chips on top - simply did not sit well.

The bus stop chitter chatter, the unwanted observations from customers in the shop, the know-all magazine and newspaper columns ranting about how life as you know it will become a distant memory well – all this made me confused, and set off a voice in my head, which screamed, "Give in! Give in!" Why did I want to fight so hard to be different? Maybe it would be better to be nestled within the bosom of other families with their screaming babies and packed off on a coach to a resort where I wouldn't feel so alone. Images of me standing in the middle of an airport tearing my hair out whilst simultaneously trying to strap my baby into a backpack, prepare formula milk and dispose of poo-filled nappies started to cloud my vision.

Luckily these feelings didn't last as Scott quickly spotted the negativity towards our free-living lifestyle that was seeping into my over-sensitive hormones. Neither my husband nor I do things by the book and Scott squashed this nonsense without ceremony. My romantic views of life after holding our new baby for the first time intact, we looked forward together to a new chapter of travelling adventures as a family.

> You simply must learn to develop a thick skin when confronted with negativity over plans to travel with a young baby. Keep a stock of phrases to hand. I particularly like to throw in the fact that my parents took a road trip right round Scandinavia with three young children in the Sixties...and survived to tell the very interesting tale. This usually shuts people up!

Why Choose Independent Travel With A Baby?

There are many moments when I feel glad we have continued our own style of travel since having Isabella, but as I write this I remember most fondly sharing a carafe of wine on the creaky balcony of a small taverna in Greece. We were watching the sun dip slowly into the sea, casting its last rays across the rough exteriors of staggered whitewashed buildings. *Bouzouki* music tinkled in the background and our laughter rained across short stubby glasses, ricocheting through the pine trees. Isabella was being cradled and cooed at by the proprietor, a healthy woman with glowing cheeks, and on that dusky evening of a family trip to the island of Skopelos, I felt that as we were experiencing new cultures, so our daughter was too. It made me feel warm inside.

Everyone has different reasons for travel. If two weeks in the sun with all food, entertainment and childcare laid on for you is what you need after a busy year hard at work, then I'm not dismissing that, but for me, wherever possible, I thrive on the complications and revelations that come from a more independent style of travel. Don't get me wrong; easy holidays are tempting when things get stressful. I love what we do, but at times it does take more stamina and the ability to grit your teeth and smile your way through some testing situations!

> If you're not sure whether independent travel is for you then consider whether you would have gone for it before becoming a parent. The odds are that if you were not up for the challenge when single, you most certainly won't be with your baby on board!

For me, though, the travel we undertake is important because I feel strongly that I want my daughter to know me as the person I am, not as an imposter changed beyond all recognition because 'that's just what happens when you have a baby'. I would be doing her an injustice by not being the person I truly want to be. Not an opinion held by everyone, but I don't see why we should change such a fundamental part of ourselves to accommodate motherhood. Granted, life develops in many new and surprising directions when you become a parent – I won't often be spotted on the dance floor of a club at 4am in the morning nowadays, preferring instead morning walks with my daughter picking wild flowers and telling her about life. But travel is something we can share and I never think, "No, we can only do that without Isabella". Instead I consider how we might arrange to do it with her.

Stored safely in my mind for the future I have vivid images of us walking knee-deep in the bright crisp snow of Northern Norway, wrapped in warm Russian hats and gloves, our rosy faces lit up with laughter against the crispest of blue skies. I see her perhaps a little older than she is now, sharing food with the smooth and exotic faces of the Far East, her mind alive with questions about a culture so different to her own. And then I see us as a family singing Elvis Presley songs at the tops of our voices with the roof down on the West Coast US road trip we have planned. What Isabella chooses to do in the future is down to her, but for now the best gift I can give is to show and share with her this vast world.

Recently I discussed with my dad, another independent traveller, what it was that made him leave his hometown in Yorkshire in search of the sights and sounds of a greater world. "I guess I was always wondering what was over that hill," he said. This is how I feel too. And for me it's not just about seeing or learning, I feel these experiences open our minds, teach us compassion, make us thankful for what we have or encourage us to change something in our own lives. The lessons are endless for Isabella and for me.

Seeing The World With Fresh Eyes

I am writing with a wide-brimmed hat shielding my eyes from the late afternoon sun, mesmerised by the view of a sparkling clear stream drifting peacefully over smooth, pale cobbles. I am aware of the faint flutters of a summer breeze making its way steadily through the trees above me and to my left I catch a glimpse – the slither of a moment – of Isabella waving Ola to a Portuguese lady. Yesterday I watched her run freely around a vineyard, making animated conversation with a pig, delighting in being allowed to sit on the mule the owner still uses to plough the land and watching with deep concentration as homemade wine was poured into stained glasses from dusty barrels in his ramshackle shed. And I realise, as we paddle in streams, split open fresh pomegranates whilst breaking from our work in a Spanish olive grove, turn our own corners to find huge lakes flanked by terracotta rock that we are learning about the innocent beauty of wonder.

You see, it's not just Isabella who is discovering the world, but through her wide and wondrous eyes I find myself re-discovering. It's like starting all over again because now when I look at something I instantly turn to her to gauge reaction. When I see her face light up in amazement it makes me look again, not with the dismissive eyes of an adult who has already seen many things, but with the eyes of a child.

> When your child looks at something, no matter how simple, look at it with them. Hold still your usual dismissive judgment that it is probably something boring and try to dig deep. Trust me when I say that it's a revelation to find yourself utterly absorbed with the antics of an ant!

I have always found beauty in small things, but with my daughter in tow, it is amplified. A field of wild flowers is not simply a pretty feast for the eyes but instead it becomes a veritable playground where we jump in, lie flat on our backs together, discover new smells and stare at the biggest sky in the world. In these pockets of time I turn to Isabella and think, "Moments like these will be printed in my memories when I am old, memories of you, of us. Like this."

Maintaining Your Adventurous Spirit

I had often wondered how becoming a mother might change my life and I had pretty much decided that in order to maintain my adventurous spirit and keep a handle on spontaneity, I might have to forgo children altogether. That was of course until the day my husband walked into my life. Funny how everything changes and becomes more attainable when you fall in love with the right person. Thus, I haven't changed – not fundamentally anyway – since having Isabella. By continuing to travel and plan to travel I have found a way to stay true to myself feeling more adventurous, if not more, as a mother. My daughter is not someone to hamper my previous life, her presence simply adds to the adventure and the things we do now as a family often turn out that bit more interesting.

In many of the European countries we have visited during the first two years of Isabella's life children are considered and valued as a new beginning, and are therefore doted on and cherished. Wherever we go a smile from Isabella can start us on a whole new adventure and I would say that we have been accepted and embraced warmly by communities because she is an ice-breaker and a talking point. I have no doubt that we have been welcomed into so many more homes and ways of life because our family unit is unthreatening. There is also the fact that as Isabella grows, so her appetite to try new things grows too, and this will push us to join her in trying new things. I don't like to show her fear – within reason – as there is such beauty in the innocence of a child who as yet does not know this emotion. Granted, I might draw the line at bungee jumping, I'm simply not that brave, but as she gets older and expresses interest in hopefully new and exciting things I may well expand and develop my own adventurous spirit with her.

When I was single I might have been scared from time to time if there was particularly bad turbulence on an aeroplane, but as I had no strong arm to cling onto or shoulder to burrow my head into, I simply dealt with it. Then I met Scott and suddenly my lovingly nurtured independent woman status drifted away in a starry-eyed haze and I made up for all of those trips alone by allowing myself to feel fear and leave unsightly nail imprints in his hand. So sue me. Anyway, now Isabella is with us I have reverted to hiding fear because I do not want her to be scared of flying, not least because it would limit our travels. Instead, by forcing myself to face things head on in my daughter's presence I am overcoming my own fear as well as encouraging her to be fearless and daring. I hope that this will lead to adventurous spirits being both maintained, and developed.

What Kind of Trip?

But then you don't necessarily have to fly to travel independently. We have walked on winding paths wild with cow parsley and buttercups, indulged recklessly in scones and clotted cream served on silver tea-stands in old-fashioned tea rooms where elderly waitresses re-live their memories with animated clarity, and watched the tide creep in on the wild North Yorkshire coast. Travel for me, no matter where, is about these moments of complete concentration. It's not about escaping from life, but about indulging in life, and our everyday routines don't always allow for this so that is why finding the time to travel, wherever or however it may be, is central to my life.

> Make snow angels. Who cares what people think. Go on woodland walks to the unknown. Be reckless; think less. You might be surprised at what you find!

For me, the thought of an all-inclusive holiday numbs my mind. I don't need to think because I'm there to switch off. There is nothing for me to wonder about, there are no decisions for me to make because the whole point of such a holiday is for ultimate relaxation. All well and good, but I thrive on doing, in locations that are unknown to me, where I feel a little out of my comfort zone and children, I have found, are far more adaptable than we might think and find true joy in the most surprising pastimes. "But what will she do to entertain herself all day in a hilltop village on a quiet Greek island?" Why, there are a million pebbles on the beach to be counted, there is dancing on the veranda of a village taverna, local children to play with. This is another surprising thing: children's ability to mix, play and communicate quickly in new situations. They just walk right in and find a way to express themselves. Just the other day we arrived at a campsite and behind the desk was a little girl the same age as Isabella. She spoke Dutch and Portuguese, but within minutes they were playing together; united over a universal cartoon character. Wherever you go, independent travels with children can prove to be an educational trip all round.

The Benefits of Pre-School Travel

The beach is empty, revealing itself in long, endless drifts of sand. We are running in circles, laughing, the crisp March air refreshing, not biting. A French family stands close by watching our kite soar into the deepest blue sky, their young son chasing after Isabella. There is nobody but Deauville locals to contend with, no sleek shiny oiled bodies clogging up the view and no extortionately-priced ice-cream vans. For me this is the beauty of pre-school travel and if you have a hankering for long-term travel too, then there is definitely no better time to head off than when your family is small.

When I left school my focus was to find work. I wanted to earn enough money to pay rent on a flat and release myself as quickly as possible from my parents and their rules. In fact, I don't think I even considered a gap year, but as the years passed I wondered if I had missed out on the freedom that comes when you just opt out of life for a while. So, when Isabella reached one and much to our own and other people's surprise, we packed up our life and headed off on the roads of France and Spain for our grown-up gap year - and what a great experience!

When it comes to long-term options travelling your child reaches school age is an excellent idea. So, if you have notions of open-ended travel and are able to give up altogether or take a sabbatical from work, start packing now!

We chose to keep our gap year fairly local due to budget and our beloved dog whom we couldn't bear to leave behind. We travelled in a camper so our accommodation and cooking facilities were sorted and along the way we volunteered on farms for fun experiences and cared for friend's houses when we tired of life in a small space. Of course, had money been no object and if we were not the adoring owners of a pampered pooch, we probably would have booked a round-the-world ticket. But, wherever you go, I cannot stress enough what a great experience long-term travel as a family offers when you don't yet have to think about schooling and all that goes with it.

> If you intend to travel long-term with your child it might be as well to wait until they are about a year old. At this point they will have had their main and most important jabs.

Before your children start school you don't need to worry about their social network or their need for security. In my opinion the only security they need is you. In addition you can wave bye-bye to inflated school holiday prices and destinations thronged with tourists. Instead you will be saying hello to restaurants filled with a handful of locals, and beaches with plenty of space, all of which is well worth the disappointment of finding out that the sun loungers have not yet been unlocked for the season. Pre-school travel of any length is great for these reasons, but long-term is wonderful and for us it proved a great bonding experience, which we see as a wonderful start to our life as a family.

Worldly Intentions

Short-term, long-term, long distance or nearer to home - hitting the road, flying afar or taking a short break as a family. Taking time out to travel together can never be a bad thing. The world is a vibrant, exciting and intoxicating place and I feel that part of my role as a mother lies in passing on to my daughter a hunger to learn about it. I relish the opportunity to teach my daughter myself in her early years and I enjoy being privy to her inquisitiveness, helping her to make sense of the world. I'm aware that she may not have distinct memories of these early travels, but these experiences will go towards forming the person she will become. Maybe Isabella will never want to travel as an adult having had enough of foreign parts. But, I hope that she will develop understanding and compassion, as well as the ability to recognise beauty in difference.

TWO

Bonjour France!
On The Road at Eight Weeks

Planning The First Road Trip

From the moment Isabella was born I found myself wondering when our first trip away together as a family would be, but it was a surprise even to me when we planned a mini road trip across France departing just eight weeks into her life. When the idea first sprang into our minds I admit a sharp intake of breath and, if the truth be known, a little butterfly fluttered quite erratically around in my tummy. A voice in my head was also nagging, questioning the sense of taking such a small bundle away from the comfort of our home. The logistics were daunting. We would be leaving behind the well-equipped changing station, the bottle-sterilising-friendly kitchen and the baby bouncer for when nothing else would do. But France would be a relatively short journey with which to launch our daughter into the world of travel and not only that, we had A Purpose.

TV programmes at the time often centred around house renovations, particularly in France, and for us the promise of a better family life with more outside space and lower house prices had captured our imagination.

This trip, therefore, was not only our first holiday as a family, but also our first peek into a world where Isabella might spend her formative years. The area we thought fitted our brief best was the Limousin due to the beautiful open countryside, charming towns and rural way of life. I did my research but as our family unit included a dog - not much more than a puppy - bouncing around, and a small baby who could potentially keep fellow guests up half the night we were quite a scary prospect for small hotel owners. Eventually I found a quaint Bed and Breakfast nestled in a quiet valley near Tulle that would accept us, and my what a relief. So, perhaps a little hastily, but bowled over with excitement that I had found somewhere, I booked.

In addition I had already started the process of obtaining Isabella's passport - and what an experience that was. The forms were picked up and read carefully front to back, several times, because they always make me nervous; am I using the wrong colour ink? Is it caps or lower case? And time was of the essence, so there was no room for mistakes. The rigorous rules for photos made me especially anxious so I decided that the easiest option would be to take Isabella in to a professional - balancing your baby in one hand whilst holding them up in a photo booth no longer cuts the mustard. Stories of babies being suspended in harnesses on the walls of photography shops scared me slightly so after some trailing around we eventually ended up in Snappy Snaps and were able to lie Isabella down flat on a large pillow, where she promptly fell asleep. The photographer assured us that it was not a problem for her eyes to be shut. Prints in hand, therefore, I marched straight to my local Post Office.

And there he was, a brusque man working his way meticulously through my paperwork behind the glass, drumming his fingers, umming and ahhing in a tone that I knew meant he was looking for a fight. Then, as if in slow motion the dreaded shake of the head and pursing of the lips started, my heart sank and I wondered what could possibly be wrong with the forms I had filled out so carefully. Maybe he was about to tell me that Isabella was too young to travel? Did he disapprove?

> **Pay extra for the Post Office to check through your application prior to sending to the passport office. Great if you're in a rush and want to make sure everything is order rather than risk them returning it to you and delaying proceedings.**

"Your daughter has her eyes closed, they will not accept this photograph," he said casually. Ahem, I'm sorry – did I hear right? "Clearly you don't have children?" I replied in my nicest voice. "I would love to know how, at two weeks old, you are able to get them to obediently open their eyes for a picture?" To which he retorted, whilst pointing vigorously at the guidelines, "I'm sorry but I am just following procedures, love, and I can tell you now that they will not accept this picture with eyes closed." I left the Post Office grumbling under my breath and thought to myself that it simply could not be right. So, I took a sneaky risk and headed to a different Post Office where the cashier agreed that it was indeed an impossibility to demand a two-week-old baby to open their eyes and sent the forms to the Passport Office with a note to that effect. A couple of weeks later, Isabella's ticket to travel dropped through the letterbox in all its beautiful and shiny glory… her photograph under the plastic page, eyes closed.

> Babies are NOT expected to have their
> eyes open for passport photos!

The Sea From A Car Seat...

...is, I suppose, a fairly serene view, but it is also seen quite differently from the eyes of parents who have suddenly understood their mistake. You see, we left Dover under dark skies and far from admiring the delicate droplets of light that danced merrily across calm and gently undulating waves, our faces were instead vacant, our brows furrowed. What had possessed us; new and sleep-deprived parents, to go for a crossing in the depths of night? When we booked, it had seemed that travelling through the night would be great for Isabella, as she would well, you know, sleep. But we had, it appeared, given little thought to our own need for some shut eye and on the boat it dawned that we had an eight-hour drive to the Limousin once we reached the other side. We were no longer the young ravers we were, and as parents our stamina could no longer take us through the night as well as the next day.

We sat on the aging velour seats stained with the stale beer of many a booze cruise, stared blankly at the carpets swirling with patterns enough to make even the most hardened tummy queasy, and watched truck drivers wandering about aimlessly with their sloshing polystyrene cups of tea before reaching the same conclusion: travel plans with a baby do indeed require a few well-though-out amendments.

> Make sure you carefully consider your own needs when planning a trip. What might have been a quite doable nighttime adventure when you were single could instead leave you looking like an extra from Thriller with your baby in tow.

But then, as the shore's lights came into view, welcoming us with their soft dusky warmth, all thoughts of what we may or may not have done wrong swiftly left our minds; we were simply glad to be getting away for a few days as a family. Sadly our physical tiredness did not evaporate with my sudden romantic appreciation of new and thrilling lands, and after 30 minutes on French roads we decided to take advantage of Isabella's continued slumbering state and pulled over for a couple of hours sleep.

> Get as much travel as you can in with a newborn; they get used to it fast, as do you and you'll learn from your mistakes quickly. Plus, it's much easier with a small bundle than it is with a toddler. Trust me!

Sleeping, Changing, Feeding... In A Car

It was not the most salubrious of locations, but we needed to rest our aching eyes. We pulled up, got as comfortable as we could and settled down. Somewhere in between the trucks that rattled hurriedly past us and refrigerated lorries that rumbled like earthquakes, we managed to grab an hour before morning began to reveal itself in thin cloudy slivers through the dark skies. A whole world began to wake up in that lay-by, and I watched silently for some precious moments before life in my own car began to unfurl. Polish truckers set out tables and chairs to enjoy breakfast together in the early sun, English drivers shared raucous banter across the parking spaces and as I opened my door to step out for a stretch, a group of young French lads working on their engine offered me a raspy bonjour, their morning cigarette smoke drifting in transparent plumes.

As always when I arrive in a new country I was consumed with the realisation that all across the world life moves along at a steady regulated pace. Sometimes it makes me wonder, "Why travel? People are doing the same things the world over." But mostly it makes me feel energised and ready to soak in the sometimes subtle, but always beautiful, differences of a new country. Strange sounds that hover, suspended in the air for brief moments as they tumble from new faces, actions that are familiar yet unusual, the smells and views of landscapes that change with varying levels of difference. And me? I have to wait, adjust to these new surroundings slowly, allowing my heart to steady until I can breathe again. Then, just on cue, Isabella began to stir in her car seat, her hands stretching out for something familiar: my face. We warmed a pre-made bottle of milk in a mug using boiled water from a flask and set off on the road, me in the back feeding a hungry Isabella.

> Take hot water in a flask to warm bottles on the go. Although many babies are completely used to room temperature milk, I think a warm bottle is comforting first and last thing.

The landscapes changed from flat patches of brown, beige and green to soft rolling valleys and along the way we decided to stop for a snack. Take time to find the designated picnic areas: these are mostly a delight, with their benches and tables, empty bins and masses of green open space, perfect for dogs, parents and children to stretch their legs. The loos however, although usually functional, often leave a little to be desired when it comes to baby changing facilities. I remembered a woman once saying to me, "I could change my son's nappy with one hand with him lying on my lap," and recalled how I wondered how this was possible. I now thought to myself that by the end of this trip I too would have it down to a tee.

We opted to start changing nappies on the back seat of the car, in a kind of production line. I would stand at the door, lay Isabella down on her mat and attempt to undress her whilst trying to stop her from rolling towards the back of the seat. Scott would pass me various items and relieve me of others. This method was adequate for now, although as we shared coffee, Isabella clean, fed and bouncing on my lap, her floppy pink sun hat shading her eyes, we agreed that we still had some way to go in achieving nappy-on-the-move perfection.

> Although I have since become a pro at one-handed nappy changing , teamwork is best. If you do not have an extra pair of hands ensure everything you need is laid out on the seat before you start. You don't want to be rooting through a bag on the floor for wipes with one hand whilst trying to ensure your baby doesn't roll off the seat with the other, in order to deal with unexpected projectile pee!

Bed & Breakfast... Baby Style

It never ceases to amaze me how the French countryside can change so gradually and yet so dramatically right before your eyes. One minute we were riding along in flat expanses of land, the next weaving through rolling hills and then out of nowhere sprang the medieval turrets of clambering stone villages balancing high above rivers in the more Northerly departments of the Limousin. We stopped for coffee in one such village, and sitting next to a cobbled market square watched locals pass the time of day, baguettes in hand. A woman wandered by, her silver hair in a bun carrying bright fresh vegetables in her basket. *"Ahh, votre fille est si paisible,"* she whispered with a smile as she saw Isabella nestled within the curve of my arm. And peaceful she was.

But it was to the Correze region in the South of the Limousin where we were headed and once again the countryside caught us unawares. Our jaws dropped at the beauty of its impressive bridges built across deep gorges and rivers, flanked with lush green foliage. After 21 hours on the road we arrived at our accommodation, hidden in a stunning valley surrounded by steep woodland and tidily planted rows of vegetables. It was certainly a welcome retreat. Our hosts offered us a cold beer in the garden before showing us to the top floor, which we had to ourselves for the price of a room. A rather clever tactical move on their part to ensure minimal disruption to other guests, I'm sure, but we were of course ecstatic about it.

The evening started peacefully with Isabella the smallest – but quietest – guest at the dinner table, and we were able to enjoy a home-cooked meal along with the other guests. Conversation came easily, wine flowed and people remarked, "How brave you are to bring Isabella away at such a young age, yet she seems so contented!" Well, you know how it goes; I probably don't even need to write it down. When someone makes a comment like that you can guarantee the abrupt end of any serenity and my how it came later that night. We retired to our floor, not too early but not too late, and lay on the bed with our daughter. There was a skylight above us, a window to a world of darkness and silence quite different from the orange glow and road noise of the city we were used to, and we slept. Peacefully. Until at some point during the night the silence was broken and Isabella's lungs let go with determined fury. We cooed, read to her, sang lullabies, but the country house seemed to come to instantaneous life anyway with doors opening and closing as guests no doubt stepped out for glasses of water, or maybe whisky. Nothing worked on Isabella and eventually we gave in to a recently acquired tactic: the car seat swing. It had started out as a new father's improvised gym workout: Isabella in her car seat being swung and lifted rhythmically and that night it was our last resort. It worked. Although any of our attempts to transfer her to bed were futile, and in the name of peace we instead placed her in the car seat into the cot.

> Putting your baby to sleep in their car seat is not a procedure that is encouraged. However, I think you will agree that in the interest of other guests it is a perfect solution!

Our reception at the breakfast table was comfortable, with lots of reassuring, "Don't worry, we've been there!" comments, but the bleary eyes and double-strength coffees told a different story. We smiled and thanked them for their understanding before shuffling out apologetically.

My New Accessory

And so we set off for our day feeling bleary-eyed ourselves, but filled with excitement at the prospect of discovering the area and looking at some properties. This part of France is typical of rural areas that are losing their young population to the big city. However, many people are now realising the potential of a country home, the French as well as buyers from other countries. The air is clear, the countryside breathtaking, scattered with waterfalls, lakes and rolling hills, and the population is small, so there is a real feeling of space. We certainly felt it was somewhere Isabella might be able to experience a childhood based around freedom and unaffected, for a while at least, by some of the more unsavoury aspects of modern life. We love the British countryside but were finding it a struggle to locate a country property within our small budget where we could raise our daughter how we wanted.

Some of the agents we met did seem baffled at our desire to traipse round houses with a tiny Isabella and our dog, but already we were a unit and planned to operate as one. The Mediterranean way, I suppose you could say, where a child is accepted as part of your family and not shooed off into the distance. I had Isabella wrapped snugly in a blanket crocheted by her Aunt in Norway, and she seemed comfortable throughout viewings. We did however make a point of breaking for the day around lunchtime to go exploring and in general Isabella was calm and contented. We always managed to find a quiet spot to rest a while for lunch and really the only disaster came when we were out and about exploring the fascinating nooks and crannies of an ancient farm building. Isabella decided it was a perfect opportunity to contribute some rather explosive and unforgiving sounds to the conversation so I promptly looked around for a bathroom before quite quickly remembering that we were in fact inside a ruin. I hastily made my excuses to the agent and left Scott in charge while I rushed Isabella to the car. However, just as I had safely laid her on the back seat and placed all the necessary equipment for the bum change operation next to her, the heavens opened and big globules of water started pelting themselves at my head through the heavy branches of the overhanging oak tree. Isabella promptly started to scream producing tears that could give the rain a run for its money and while all this was going on I had the most unpleasant nappy to deal with. I tried to remain calm, of course, but in some situations it is almost impossible, so when I re-appeared 20 minutes later my face was red and the rain gleamed sweatily on my skin. Scott took one look, and quite quickly we were on our way back to the Bed and Breakfast to watch the rain pitter patter on the skylight softly.

Stuck In Paris Traffic On The Road Home

There had been no theme parks or flash restaurants and we had not found a place we would be willing to give up our life in the UK for, but our family unit enjoyed these few days together and despite other people's opinions, had even found it relaxing. Although this changed a little when, as we were happily rolling along the tree-lined avenues in Paris remarking on stately homes and wondering where to stop for a very Parisian coffee, the midday heat began to interfere with our otherwise serene morning drive.

I was designated the map reader, and I didn't yet have our faithful TomTom navigation system to help me out. Don't get me wrong, it's a running joke with my dad that I have found my way around various tricky destinations such as Bangkok, Granada and the Greek Isles in a car with little more than a hand-drawn map on the front seat and a bit of savvy. But maybe motherhood had sucked some of that sense from me, because suddenly Scott was remarking in a, "I'm trying to be nice but you are utterly rubbish at map reading," voice. "Babe, this doesn't seem right to me, are you sure we are on the right road?" I replied, matter-of-factly, "Well that is what the map is telling me, maybe you would like to swap?" You see, my husband is the worst passenger in the world; he literally hates not driving, whereas I am not bothered either way, so that's the deal. He drives, I try to read maps and we keep out of each other's way when it comes to making decisions. Well, that is unless heat begins to seep in and tempers begin to flare.

"OK, but there is a traffic jam ahead," he remarked hurriedly. I glared. "So is that my fault?" Silence. At this point the sun was scorching, we were stuck in traffic, possibly lost and now my new mother hysteria kicked in to tell me that Isabella and Milla may be cooking in the car. We drove on making little progress until we decided to pull over so that I could climb into the back and administer cool flannels. Our daughter looked decidedly un-phased by the events but that didn't stop me from worrying. She is now two-and-a-half and I still check to make sure she's breathing in the middle of the night and just the other day I remarked to my friend that, "Maybe I'll still be doing this when she's 16!" Anyway, at some point we managed to turn off the main road and although the sunshine remained, our stress levels thankfully decreased, possibly with heat exhaustion. Soon we were enjoying a slow amble back to the port of Calais singing Elvis songs at the tops of our voices - a divorce successfully averted.

> Try not to drive through or round busy cities in the heat of the day with your baby on board. They will probably take it in their stride, but you will be at risk of injecting unnecessary tension into your relationship!

On the boat back to the UK we concluded that our first family trip had been a resounding success. We had learnt so much, not least that most of the clothes we had brought for our little one were unnecessary, and that we had taken far too many nappies – not that it matters when you have space in the car on a road trip, but for a flight we realised 80 nappies were perhaps too many. We patted each other on the back in praise of our newfound one-handed nappy changing skills but agreed that choosing to stay at a small Bed & Breakfast with a newborn was probably unfair to the other guests.

For us, though, our first foray into family travel proved mainly to be the beginnings of a truly bonding experience where we all had the time to take notice of each other and we especially loved that Milla had taken to resting her head on Isabella's car seat, as if she was taking care of her. We may not have found our dream home or left France feeling convinced that living abroad was for us, but we were already making plans for our next voyage!

Babies exist the world over. You don't need to stuff hundreds of nappies in your suitcase; just pick up them up at a local chemist.

THREE

Mama Mia!

Flying Greek at Three Months

The Skies Are Blue

The skies are blue, pure and still as I look to my right out of the window. Thin slithers of white cloud rest delicately mid-air and the hum of the engine drowns out the hostess asking fellow passengers if they would like a drink. Repetitive niceties drift in and out of my mind as I sit, staring out of the window, my small baby sleeping peacefully on my chest. Eventually the trolley reaches me. "Awww, how old is she?" the blonde and perfectly groomed hostess whispers. "Three months," I reply with a silent thought that I really should get my nails done. "Oh, she is so good!" A smug smile sits on my face as I remember how I would often be flying solo watching other parents struggling with their screaming children. I thought about how I intended my daughter to be different and that by the time she was two she would be a professional and not bat an eyelid at traversing continents in big hunks of metal. Of course, as you make your way through this book you will realise that just because you get your children used to travel at a young age, it does not mean that they will always perform how you want them to or that they will be the plane-hopping businessman or romantic couple's dream. But for now, let me bask in the glory that is the adorable travelling baby.

> I think it is the biggest misconception that short-haul plane travel with a newborn is difficult. They will normally sleep peacefully in your arms whilst joyously lapping up milk as and when needed, in particular at fractious moments. Wait until they are that bit older and you'll be wrestling with a boisterous child who requires constant stimulation, whether they are used to travel or not.

It is true that our darling daughter was the picture perfect baby on our first trip through Mediterranean skies and we felt so utterly thankful that it was pain free because we dreaded everyone else tutting in disgust. We even had the nappy changing down to a tee, again opting for the two-person approach as attempting to master it alone in such a small place, although doable, is fairly stressful and requires forward-thinking combined with the ability to use your mouth, hands, feet and arms simultaneously; a challenge, especially when you are aware of a growing queue of people standing outside. So, one of us would enter with Isabella and place her on the very tiny changing shelf; the other would pass items in when required. Just like the car method, only at 35,000 feet, which let me tell you is no easy feat when combined with the occasional jolt of turbulence to add to the adventure, but after a couple of goes you do get the hang of it!

> Note that fellow passengers are mostly a lot more understanding when you are on a flight to a holiday destination. You might get a few looking over in disgust, but you're normally pretty safe from single businessmen and women who really seem to hate travelling near tots.

Of course, it was embarrassing when Isabella decided to go all out with the emptying of her bowels and as the air-hostess waited patiently outside for us to finish before heading off with her drinks trolley, her perfectly made-up face did grimace ever so slightly in disgust. Overall, though, it was a success and as we touched down and left the plane to the mild blue Greek skies we felt a sense of euphoria that plane travel was still to play a big part in our lives.

Taxi, Boat, Bus... Bring it on!

Arriving at Skiathos airport is a typically Greek experience that could quite easily be a scene from the movie My Big Fat Greek Wedding – I hope you get the picture. It's small, everyone is bumbling around trying to retrieve their bags from the only luggage carousel, the sound of raised voices bounces off the walls in echoing mayhem, people gesture wildly, and guards recline nonchalantly with cigarettes and a blatant lack of concern for any mishaps that may be unfolding around them. It is unstructured, to say the least and when I first arrived at this airport in 2002 as a travel researcher, I was charmed. Fast forward to the present day - with a tiny Isabella packed tightly against me in a sling, a buggy under one arm and a rucksack, it was slightly less enchanting. But with a deep breath and the silent mantra, "Of course I can travel with a baby". I soldiered on.

> Slings are a great option for travel when your baby is small.
> Attempting to fold and unfold your buggy whilst trying to remove
> or strap in your baby and hail a taxi is a nightmare. Strap your
> baby to you as soon as you exit the plane and keep them there –
> it will also give you peace of mind when it comes to the taxi...

As we exited the terminal building we were hit square on by the June heat. We wasted no time, however, and marched straight across the road as we knew we needed to start queuing for a taxi immediately. There are always far more people than taxis outside this airport and everybody is desperate to get to the port to catch connecting ferries to the surrounding islands. There is no real system for cab hailing or waiting. Whoever can get out into the road and gesticulate enough to capture the eye of the taxi driver gets to ride first. *"Yasas! Yasas!"* Scott shouted whilst beckoning me over to stand with him in the road thus demonstrating to the driver that there is a baby out in the heat who is probably about to get crushed in the rush or suffer dehydration if he does not save us. Right this minute. No pressure of course. Oh I know, it's probably cruel and irresponsible to of me to use my daughter as a tool to get in there first and admittedly we – in our pre-parenting life – had tutted and raised our eyebrows in disgust at people who did the same. But with sweat dripping down our faces, Isabella ready for milk, a ferry to catch pronto, and neither of us enthralled by the thought of occupying her for another few hours whilst waiting for the next crossing, desperate measures were needed. I stepped forward and played the knackered and concerned mother role as best I could. It worked a treat. I mean, who wants to deal with a stressed and potentially angry new mother? The taxi driver stopped slap bang in the middle of the road and loaded our bags into the car before shouting to see if there was another couple wanting to join the party. Let me warn you – things are different in Greece. All health and safety goes out of the window and you must leave your own thoughts about rules and regulations firmly back in your country of origin. So, there we were; our luggage loosely secured with an old belt in the half-open boot of the taxi, me strapped in the back with Isabella close to me in her sling, Scott in the front doing his best to make Greek small-talk with the driver and a couple in the back, their two boys aged about five and seven happily on their laps.

It's a short ride down a dusty, bumpy track to the harbour where the hustle and bustle of a tourist sunshine destination stirs itself into a fury. Bright lights, music, scantily-clad tanned couples parading up and down the promenade on scooters, Greece in the summertime is careless living at its best. Our destination was more off the beaten track and more subdued, so instead, after swiftly downing a much-needed ice-cold Mythos beer in a café where the young waitress and her friends cuddled and cooed over Isabella, we bought our ferry tickets and waited to board the boat to Loutraki, Skopelos. Struggling onto a packed boat filled with Greek locals returning from the mainland, their huge purchases in hand, can be quite a hectic and sweaty experience, which is why a sling is essential. I had the hand luggage rucksack on my back, Isabella on my front, while Scott shoved the backpack and buggy safely into the right cubbyhole. Of course, if I'm travelling alone then it's just a case of not being so extravagant with packing and I can assure you it is still possible to deal with a buggy, a backpack and a baby. Soon enough we were on the boat watching the heat of the day sizzle and evaporate on the calm seas. Putting myself mentally there now I feel a serenity wash over me. It's so truly mesmerising. The deep blue sea, jagged silver rocks thrusting up into a still sky, white-washed buildings perched precariously on hillsides, the steady hum of the engine and some terrible Greek soap opera on the TV. Admittedly the last component adds an unusual aspect, but nonetheless it is a comforting moment. And then before we knew it Loutraki port came into view dominated by our destination: the hopelessly romantic village of Glossa that rests high above.

> When travelling with your baby forget suitcases. A large backpack is much more transportable and easier to handle.

Delicate lights decorate the hillside, strung across in wavy lines, inviting you up to winding cobbled streets flanked by traditional houses and the odd taverna hidden through a small doorway or at the top of a secret staircase. We had fallen in love with the Sporades islands on a previous trip to Alonissos back in 2004 but we had since discovered the charms of Skopelos and the village of Glossa; a perfect getaway from modern life. It is traditional, peaceful and very beautiful, due to the lush green terrain that dominates despite the heat. In fact the island itself was chosen to become the backdrop of the Mama Mia movie and every time I watch the film I fall in love all over again with its craggy rocks that descend into the seas and as I close my eyes I can almost smell the marjoram and mint and see the wild poppies. Sadly I wonder if having become home to such a blockbuster it might well have lost some of its charms. I haven't been back since the film, but I do hope it has not given in to Abba tourism, although I'm certain that Glossa itself will have remained out of the glare of Skopelos town.

The boat chugged into the port, we disembarked and made our way to the bus stop with a sleeping Isabella. It's a 15-minute uphill ride to Glossa along a winding road that within moments has you looking down on the quaint church and tavernas of Loutraki, a good place for a stroll, but not a patch on Glossa. The bus eventually came to a standstill outside the tobacconist at the bottom of the village - most of Glossa is pedestrianised. We stepped off and sauntered up the hill, stopping for a carafe of *krasi* (wine) at the Souvlaki, the heart of this village. Small tables and rickety chairs on a stone walled terrace, blue and white checked tablecloths, raucous laughter from locals. Some friends squealed with delight as they saw us arrive with our new addition; keen to welcome her in true Greek fashion. Despite her long journey she lapped up the attention with grace, offering the odd gurgle and ahhh at just the right time. Drinks were toasted and laughter crackled through the night air before it fizzled out with tiredness and we headed to our house: a one up, one down bijou affair in a slightly crumbling but beautiful street. We arrived, opened all the shutters to let in some cool night air and put missy straight to bed in her bubble.

> The single best investment that I urge you to make if you want your baby to be super transportable is a Samsonite pop up bubble cot. We have used it for numerous dinner parties and taken it with us on holidays (it will fit in your luggage or can be taken as hand luggage) and for the little one it has proved a home from home.

Little Swimmer

That night we slept like logs - not difficult in Glossa. The only noises you hear in the night are the sounds of mopeds softly buzzing around the car-free streets, crickets rubbing their wings together in the still air and the odd strum of Greek music floating up from closing tavernas. And because Isabella is so at home in her bubble we didn't hear a peep from her until the early morning. We rose, showered, unpacked and then headed to the café for a pastry and a *frappa* before embarking on the scenic walk to the chapel of St. John sto Kastri.

> A Factor 50 beach tent is a great idea. Buy a pop-up one as these are small enough to fit in your luggage and are perfect if your baby wants a rest on the beach. They can get quite warm inside so still try to pitch them under a little shade.

You can walk 30 minutes to the port of Loutraki for a swim, which is very pleasant and perfect for your daily dip, but if you want something more breathtaking then it has to be St John's. Just out of the village you take a turn toward the opposite side of the island and walk downhill for a good hour. It is easy to think you won't get anywhere, but my how it is worth it in the end! Before we became parents we would always hire a moped to get around the island, but a small baby puts this out of the question, so walking it was. Having said that, when we stayed on Alonissos we were waiting to hire a bike behind a couple just finalising their deal. They had a young son, all of about three years old, and to our amazement hired a bike and one helmet; they put it on his head, and got on with him squished in the middle. We stood there open-mouthed and tried to imagine how this would go down in the UK, but here it's really nothing unusual. Highly illegal and potentially hugely dangerous, I am sure, but fun - and it least it's not as bad as Thailand. In Bangkok the children don't even have helmets and hang precariously on the back wearing little more than wide and captivating smiles, amidst the most haphazard traffic jams I have seen in my life. It was difficult enough for me to try and navigate this city on four wheels in the first place, but the addition of bikes transporting whole families weaving themselves into my already muddled route stopped my heart a million times. At least on Skopelos the roads are quiet and the road to St. John's is as silent as can be for what seems like hours. Suddenly the sea appears, vast and glistening up ahead, rocks jutting out here and there, higgledy piggledy steps leading down to a small cove where you can while away the hours paddling and looking at fish in the rock pools and swimming out to dive off the rocks. The monastery is to your left at the top of a hundred or so steps perched dangerously on a solitary rock. No wonder this became the backdrop to the wedding in Mama Mia – I can think of no prettier place and I'm certain that as I type this there is many a romantic couple trying to convert to the Greek Orthodox religion so they can get wed there themselves.

We were not there to get married, but to enjoy basking in the sunny waters of this magical place - and no-one loved it more than Isabella. She absolutely adores the water. Comfortable in her swim pants, a kind of costume with cloth waterproof lining, she was happier than ever to be dipped in and out of the water and when she needed a nap we placed her in a factor 50 beach tent, a great find recommended by Scott's hairdresser. When she was tiny we could pop her in there knowing she was shielded from harmful rays and happily read our books for an hour or two. Make the most of this because the time when you are still able to lounge on the beach and forget you have a baby is limited.

> Little Swimmer nappies or waterproof swimming knickers are perfect for your baby. They can splash around to their heart's content without you worrying about them leaving a present for fellow bathers! We also found that the nappies can in fact be dried and reused... if they are clean of course!

Of course, all enjoyment must be balanced with a little hard work, and the only problem with holidaying on this amazing island is that what goes down must come up again. When you head to St Johns, you must not forget to take a taxi number with you to get you back up with ease. There are no buses from this wild and more rugged side of the island and walking back is pretty tough – especially with the addition of a buggy, made for mountains or not. We had *Yanni's* number to hand so with an unbroken sense of peace and tranquillity, we returned to our house at a leisurely pace just in time for a mid-afternoon beer on the balcony.

> When it comes to the beach we always try to get out first thing in the morning. By the time the heat really starts to get up you want to be safely in the shade of your balcony enjoying a beer while your baby takes an afternoon nap.

Gimme, Gimme ,Gimme Milk After Midnight

In countries like Greece you have to embrace a different lifestyle. In England it is not commonplace to go out in the evening for a meal or to a bar and expect to see children running around but in Glossa parents do not venture out unless their children are in tow so having a baby in a pushchair at a restaurant is not a problem. Our favourite restaurant in Glossa, Maistrali, did not bat an eyelid at carrying Isabella in her buggy up the steps before clearing a space for her on the terrace, fantastic view thrown in for free, and when it came to her dinner we simply asked for a bowl of hot water in which to warm up her milk.

> I'm pretty certain that any restaurant in Greece will be happy to provide a bowl of hot water for you to warm your baby's bottle in – don't be afraid to ask!

There are two restaurants in Glossa that stand out but it is Agnanti that gets all the praise. This is the famous long-standing family restaurant that entices the rich from their yachts, which dock frequently at Loutraki during Mediterranean cruises, but for us it is Maistrali that offers better views, and the food and service are just as good. After our dinner of zucchini balls, fresh greens and a dish made with local plums, we strolled around the village and found ourselves pulled into the schoolhouse taverna for a late night drink. It's a bit more spit and sawdust but locals loiter here so you get a real feeling of life on the island. It is with these impromptu stops in mind that I urge you to always have enough bottles made up for your baby, as you never know when you will need to pacify screams. In particular I rate readymade cartons, which have proved a godsend on more than one occasion. I would always pack a few for emergencies, such as when I was tucking into deliciously succulent stuffed vine leaves and Isabella started to unexpectedly wail. Her nighttime feed already devoured I looked around in desperation before whipping one such carton from my handbag and decanting it swiftly in to her bottle so that peace would quickly be resumed. Nothing should come between a mother and her vine leaves!

> **Always pack a few ready-made milk cartons if you're not breast-feeding. They are perfect if you're caught out unawares.**

Before we set off on this trip, one of the things I worried most about was sterilising bottles. When you're at home you become so consumed with how many baby products and gadgets you need in your life that I think it is easy to lose perspective about what is actually necessary. People have been having babies for many thousands of years and it is good to remind yourself of this from time to time and I dare say that sterilising bottles with boiling water is probably sufficient. However, we did take with us some sterilising tablets and then all we had to do was buy a big bowl, fill it with water, drop in a tablet and plunge in the bottles. You can do this wherever you are. We also bought our milk formula at a local chemist to save on packing space. Granted I have a smattering of Greek so could read most of the label and with the addition of a good dictionary and a local man who just happened to have lived in America for many years and thus spoke perfect English, we knew what we were buying was OK for Isabella.

> To save on packing do try local formula milk from the chemist. It's nothing to be scared about and you will often recognise International brands. Never fear – there will always be someone who can help you out and failing that, never leave home without a good dictionary! Also remember to take some sterilising tablets, which can be dropped straight into a bowl of cold water.

That first family holiday to Greece was a dream, enjoyed by us all. We remember the pale, dark and royal blues, emerald green leaves that ruffled in soft breezes, food that left our lips softly oiled and our stomachs comfortably content. Walks where we would just stop still to soak up the sea views, look at wild flowers and enjoy the abundant smells. Strolls through cobbled streets stopping for a coffee where men played board games and women dressed in black cooed over Isabella from their front steps and verandas, their weathered faces telling many a story about their own life as mothers. None of these events seemed less than they would have been before Isabella; in fact I think we were welcomed even more. Yes, as a first air trip with a small baby, it was enough to remind us that the worries about travel with children are often unfounded.

FOUR

Ahoy Captain!

Magical Norway at Eight Months

Beautiful Bergen

Beautiful Bergen captured me within moments and this was despite the fact that my eyes were under the veil of night skies. There was a crispness to the air and as I closed my eyes and breathed in, a fairy tale feeling whooshed under my nose that made me think of mysterious fishermen's stories unravelling in a sea breeze. I had experienced this feeling before when I first visited a Scandinavian country working for the tourist guide, only that time it had been Denmark. Sitting on a bench in Copenhagen I wrote in my notebook about the Little Mermaid: "She seems the most unlikely of tourist attractions, sitting small and feeble on her stone amongst the soft ripples of the sea. She looks away from her admirers in a way that is sad, no doubt longing for her Prince." Granted, I do like to get lost in the moment, but even then I was taken with the sense of magical intrigue (something to do with Hans Christian Andersen I'm sure) that hangs heavy over this part of the world and I had vowed to explore Scandinavia further. Luckily for me my brother has since fallen in love with Norway, and a Norwegian girl, and thus I was delivered to Northern skies once again, to celebrate my 32nd birthday, this time with my family in tow.

We had arrived at the airport at night with my sister and her husband and as we walked through the glass corridor above the arrivals hall I saw my brother and his girlfriend waving frantically and I held Isabella up so we could wave back. The flight had been a breeze with no real hiccups - at eight months Isabella had become a pro. We sat in the departures lounge and enjoyed a pub dinner before our flight and apart from a few tears at takeoff and landing, the spell in between had been relatively calm. The beauty of a later departure is that you can time it around milk and sleep, ensuring a restful flight.

> With flights do your best to book one around nap or evening sleep time. There is nothing better than being able to give your baby a bottle at take-off and then watch them slip into a slumber for the rest of the flight. Make sure you go to the loo first though as you will not want to disturb your baby once they drift off!

Bergen is a city and as with any city there is lots going on, but this one is smaller and more friendly than many I have visited. Not only that, but as we set out first thing to meet up in the centre with the rest of the gang we were able to fully appreciate its setting. It rests within seven spectacular mountains, pretty colourful buildings with pointed roofs staggering right down to the ocean's edge. I could immediately see why my brother loves the place because it has all you expect from a city, yet within moments you can get away from it all – a sort of easily-accessed freedom, ideal for us free-spirit types.

Café Culture & The View From The Top

I had been looking forward to this trip for a while and had been wondering how we would fare with Isabella in tow. I knew that nights out on the town would be out; she was getting too big to conceal in a trendy handbag. Only kidding of course. But I was keen to find out how restaurants took to eight-month-olds in this part of the world and I did have my concerns that she would become frustrated in a city. Taking a baby to the beach or vast open fields and letting them crawl wildly is one thing, but expecting them to stay contented while parents indulge in a bit of city culture might be a bit much for a now slightly more wriggly and demanding baby. I didn't need to worry.

> When your baby comes out of their newborn stage you need to make sure there is plenty to keep them occupied if you expect them to stay happy and congenial while you're knocking back cappuccinos and conversation with friends. I find that a little rucksack containing books, a pull along toy and various other bits and bobs works a treat, for a while anyway.

Café Culture is big in this city and as this is a part of the world not famed for blazing hot sunshine and we were visiting in November, our weekend was spent strolling casually around cobbled streets before nipping into quirky cafes for tea (in teacups), coffee and *blings*, which consisted of one slice of bread with a generous amount of topping. I know, I know, it's a hard life. What I learned on this trip is that Isabella was easily amused and not at all a problem. At eight months she was fascinated by everything, and could and would eat most things, which made her easy to pacify. With a doting aunt or uncle in front of her for entertainment well, she was charming. She sat with us in cafes quite comfortably on squishy sofas, wooed waiters and waitresses with her big eyes, drank milk gleefully and was happy to show customers her cheeky smile and her toys. The only downside? Quirky cafes may not be equipped with fancy baby changing facilities and often a tiny unisex toilet with minimal floor space at the top of a creaky staircase is as good as it's going to get. If the floor looked passable, which they mostly did, I would whip out my portable changing mat and when it didn't, well it was a case of sitting on the loo and doing it one-handed, and I'm afraid there is not room for two in these places. Anyway, Isabella certainly didn't seem to be a hindrance on our café tour to anyone in the party. In fact I think she added to the day's activities and when it came to nap time we strapped her into the mountain buggy, undid the zippers to switch it to sleep mode and continued on our stroll.

> If you intend to travel as you did prior to your baby you will find that some changing facilities are basic to say the least. Please, please, please make sure you pack a portable changing mat.

After our leisurely morning and lunchtime activities, we took a stroll by the water's edge where fishermen waited patiently for their lunch, tall trees swayed in the November winds and hidden totem poles jumped out on us with spooky hilarity and eventually the winding path led us to the Aquarium. This woke our little girl up instantly and pressing her nose against the glass to see penguins eye to eye kept her busy and content for quite some time. In fact, I think the only tears on that trip came when we tried to tear her away. It is so important to balance things out when your baby gets a little older on travels. OK, so they are pretty good at being amused with teaspoons in cafes, but then you need to do something that is utterly engaging for them, too. For me this approach works a treat; I get to do what I want to do with minimal hassle and then at the same time we get to do something that Isabella is enthralled by. Besides, by the end of the Aquarium visit all of us grownups were wondering why we hadn't visited such a place in so long. You see, what did I say earlier about seeing the world through your child's eyes? You get to grow up all over again!

Another thing you absolutely must do when you visit Bergen is view it from the top of Mount Floyen, reached by the rather flashy vertical funicular train that we managed to cram the buggy onto, with Isabella firmly strapped in. It's a pretty cool journey up and the fantastic views of Bergen and surrounding islands are well worth a look. Seeing a city from above is fascinating, as it gives a whole new perspective, often completely different from when you are within its streets, encompassed by its buildings and shadowed by its people. I have seen many a city from high up but in particular I always reminisce about Bangkok. Walking out of the airport in a daze I jumped straight into a taxi, which took me directly to my hotel. Other than a few fleeting glances at people cooking their dinner over stoves under flyovers and young men stretching their dark limbs into the fading sun on their cramped terraces, I hadn't really looked around me enough to comprehend the size of the place. It wasn't until I arrived in my hotel room that I stopped to look out of the window and as I gulped deeply I thought, "How am I ever going to go out there and find anything?" I'm not ashamed to say that as a single woman with a full schedule that would see me traversing this city alone for six days, I felt fear. It was vast, towering, scary and seemed like an impossible landscape to navigate with little more than a notebook and a street map. However, once I was walking under wooden balconies, strolling amidst colourful side stalls and hopping on and off river taxis, it felt much smaller. The fear subsided, to quickly be replaced with a strange sense of enjoyment at my ability to negotiate a place so different to all I had known. So while Bergen may not be so dissimilar to my native land, and the view of wild seas and islands cloaked in mist less daunting than the views of Bangkok, seeing a city from above is recommended because it does give a completely different perspective. Bergen looked bigger and more spread out than I had expected, a far cry from the quaint, pretty and colourful lanes we had been strolling through, not to mention that the journey up and the consequent photo opportunities of Isabella in a hat, Isabella in a blanket, Isabella with Auntie, Isabella with Mummy… kept things peaceful.

Out On The Town & In Search of Cheap Wine

One thing you must be prepared for in Norway is that it is certainly not cheap. As a Brit, for me to say that is quite unusual. So be prepared for this because if you're thinking of seeing this city on a budget you could be in for a shock. In my case I am lucky; my brother lives there and he and his girlfriend very kindly put us up in their flat while they stayed at her parents, so we were able to settle into our own family's routine and make our own entertainment as necessary.

Consider self-catering accommodation when visiting a city as it provides a home-from-home environment for you and your baby and means that you can work out an itinerary to your own rules.

Isabella was in routine from a few months old simply because our lifestyle - me working from home as well as being a full-time mum - meant that I needed to know, pretty much, when I would get time to do things that needed to be done. In some ways this worked for us, but in other ways it worked against us. On the plus side we could plan things well when Isabella was a baby but when those plans went out of the window, which they of course did from time to time, it was not the most enjoyable situation. Just this happened that evening. After our busy day sightseeing we all agreed to meet back in town for dinner with my brother set to pick us up at 6pm. We rushed back, had showers and prepared Isabella for our evening out, minus her night-time bottle. We knew that this way, by the time we came to sit down at the restaurant at 7pm, it would be the perfect time to leave her in her buggy with a bottle of milk, so that she would fall happily into a silent slumber. We would be able to enjoy our meal in peace, which – given the cost of food and alcohol - was very important indeed. But alas, as we sat waiting, watching the clock, texting and phoning my brother to no avail, Isabella started to get grizzly. It was by now 6.45pm and we knew that our window to settle her to sleep was very quickly slipping away. By the time my brother eventually phoned, explaining that they had fallen asleep, I was seething because I knew our peaceful meal was now extremely unlikely. But by the time he arrived to collect us, I had realised that my annoyance was possibly more to do with envy of their ability to have an impromptu nap!

When we arrived at the restaurant Isabella had of course passed the point of tiredness that would take her to sleep, and took a while to settle. The proprietors were fabulous; no fuss about bringing the buggy in, warm water supplied in a bowl for her bottle and fellow diners didn't bat an eyelid even when she complained loudly at the change to her routine. The meal was still good, although the drink was expensive, so we decided that the best plan of action was to go in search of cheap wine and head back to the apartment. A cheap bottle of wine in a Norwegian off-licence costs as much as a house wine in a restaurant in England, but it was nice to retreat back to our accommodation, pop Isabella into her bubble and natter away into the small hours.

Out On The Boat

It was the purest of skies, not a single cloud interrupting the cool blue. Cold, but the kind of crisp bracing cold that makes a person feel alive. On that, the morning of my birthday, I stood silently, holding Isabella in my arms and watching the port of Bergen merge backwards into the embrace of its surrounding mountains, listening to the converted fishing-to-diving boat's engine chug along rhythmically beneath me, and I thought: "I will always remember this moment and this birthday."

The diving boat my brother used to work on as an instructor; come cook, come man about deck, just happened to be docked in Bergen port at the time of our visit so my brother jumped aboard to sweet-talk his old boss – a rather hilarious, no-nonsense Yorkshireman –

into taking us for a spin in the Norwegian seas. Possibly swayed by the thought of birthday cake, he quietly agreed. It was truly magical. Just moments out of town felt a million miles away, somewhere lost in time, where the sea is not the azure of the Mediterranean, but instead a rich deep royal blue. Where cabins cling to rocks and the air is silent, smooth and clean; the perfect remedy for a sore head after a boozy night and an early wake-up call. Isabella, oblivious to our hangovers, was happy to snooze in her buggy on deck, basking in the late November sun, wrapped up in a thick Puffa jacket, another blanket made by her Auntie along with various mittens, hats and scarves. This trip taught me quickly that trying to get a small baby into winter accessories can be tricky and I was certainly not always convinced that Isabella was warm enough – I now know that a snow suit is the answer.

> **When you are travelling somewhere cold, the best item of clothing I can recommend taking is an all-in-one all weather suit.**

It was wonderful to be on the boat my brother had worked on for several years, see the small bunk he lived in below decks, meet the Skipper I had heard so much about and realise just how scary it must have been to be thrown in at the deep end, having to sail across the North Sea from Scotland through the night. Certainly not something I could ever do - when the boat seemed to be rocking quite significantly my brother announced that on a scale of 1-10, this was minus! And although this voyage into the North Sea was taken fairly well by my daughter, a jaunt in more treacherous weather might have been a step too far for her, too. The rest of the afternoon was a relaxing combination of eating cake and soaking up the stunning scenery. A wonderful time was had by all, not least the birthday girl, and it was with reluctance that we turned back towards the port and watched our time in Norway drift to a watery close.

My thirst for magical Scandinavia could not be quenched in one short weekend and I was left with grand ideas of next time taking a train further north, into the Arctic Circle, maybe with a toddler Isabella wrapped up in a ski suit. For me, this part of the world – so near to some of the most extreme locations on our planet – offers excitement and a feeling of exploration and although we would like to visit in summer, I feel that the winter weather does add something more to the experience; offering days that leap straight from the pages of children's adventure stories.

FIVE

Greece By All Means...
A Whistlestop Tour

Planning The Long Journey

Isabella was a year old when we decided to travel the long way round to Skopelos, with a whistle stop tour of Athens thrown in for good measure. As she was still at an age where school was not an issue we made the decision to travel out of season. Skopelos in season means a charter flight to the neighbouring island of Skiathos followed by a short boat-ride and maybe the odd taxi journey. Out of season involves embarking on the longer, more varied itinerary, via Athens. We were a little daunted about how we would all cope with an early morning London Gatwick flight to Athens, a metro from the airport to the centre, a three-hour bus ride from there to the port of Aghios Constantinos, followed by a three-hour boat ride to Skopelos, and finally a taxi to Glossa. But, nothing ventured nothing gained and we agreed that we were all ready to take on this complicated travel itinerary and saw it as a great opportunity to enjoy some more of this vast and varied country in a short space of time.

On such a long trip the main thing we were worried about was keeping Isabella entertained. A bored, restricted one-year-old can and will scream the plane, bus, train or boat down if they feel like it and we knew that this was much more likely to happen if Isabella was tired. Our Easyjet flight was like the budgie – cheap – with the unsociable departure time of 6am, so we opted for a very reasonably-priced hotel room at Gatwick so we could all get a good sleep. By 7pm we would be watching a movie, tucked up in a giant bed with crisp white sheets, giving us our best chance of a fairly happy Isabella and thus a wonderfully serene mummy and daddy ready to take on an 18 hour trip to Greece.

> We no longer attempt to stay up all night in order to make early departures. This is best left to Ibiza-bound party people and I strongly suggest that you accept this fact sooner than we did.

Another thing we thought a lot about was packing. Trying to negotiate various modes of transport, zipping in between each, usually in a rush with a baby who is screaming for milk, snacks or a nappy change, can be pretty hairy with mountains of baggage. Forget the vanity case and stack of suitcases and pack for maximum portability. Think lean. I spent my teens trying to not turn into my mother, but as an adult I realise she has a lot of savvy and I can now say that one of the most important things I have learnt from her is that in life we all need a list! This is essential because although some unnecessary item will always makes it into your luggage, there will most certainly be less than if you packed without one. We managed this trip with one large back-pack, two hand-luggage rucksacks and a buggy with cot attached to it. I know that lots of you will be travelling to accommodation that will provide a cot, but if you are not, then this combination works well.

> We use a Mountain Buggy when we travel. It's essential for Skopelos terrain, doubles up as somewhere for your baby to sleep, and we can strap the bubble cot to it in transit, thus getting away with loading them both into the hold! (Normally you are limited to one cot or one buggy.)

So, as prepared as we could be and armed with a healthy dollop of positive thinking, and a slightly manic excitement for what would be Isabella's longest and most varied travel itinerary to date, we drove to our airport hotel in the afternoon, ordered pizza and chilled out until the alarm woke us from our slumbers at 3am, when we trundled off down the dimly lit corridor in search of warmer climes.

> When you're heading off on a trip with lots of changes and modes of transport, you need to take as few clothes as you can. For Isabella we packed a small selection of outfits, a Kagool, several sleepsuits and then we layered her in really warm clothes for the plane. Always work out how many outfits you can realistically hand-wash and get dry.

Away We Go... How To Enjoy Wine On A Plane

Without a doubt the one thing that helped us on our long journey to Greece was bagging extra seats both on the way there and on the way back. Now I'm not sure if it makes me a bad mother or a resourceful one, but when travelling I have been known to use Isabella as a decoy in order to manipulate a situation. Taking your baby on a plane, especially when they are no longer that small, can be a daunting prospect. There you are with said child on your lap and not only do you have to feed, comfort, burp and entertain them without tears, which even in the comfort of your own home may not be struggle free, but you have to do so in a tiny confined space. When your baby finally does fall asleep you are then unable to move for fear of waking them and having to start the whole process again. In this situation parents are left with the prospect of no loo, no snack and in my case, certainly no option for a trashy novel and a glass of wine. This is what gets me in the holiday spirit and drives me to do my darnedest to get another seat and as I can guarantee that it will make your flight much easier, let me share our approach with you.

> Getting an extra seat for your baby is really a bonus that is worth some extra work! The extra space is a godsend when it comes to manoeuvrability for all.

If you travel budget like us you will find that on some airlines, seating is 'free' – this means you don't have a seat number. These are also usually the aeroplanes with minimal leg-room so our modus operandi is that first, we take advantage of the fact that passengers with children get to board first and we leg it down to the plane, Isabella tightly in my arms, Scott in charge of dumping the buggy on route without knocking the attendant flying. We then rush to the back of the plane and sit ourselves each in an aisle and a window seat, Isabella in the middle, take a deep breath and wait for fellow passengers to start boarding, at which point we throw Isabella up in the air with glee, make her giggle – loudly – and generally attempt to do anything that alerts boarding passengers to the fact that WE HAVE A VERY YOUNG BABY HERE WHO IS LIABLE TO SCREAM AND MAKE LOTS OF NOISE AND POTENTIALLY UPSET YOUR CALM FLIGHT.

Think about a time Before Babies… there you are looking forward to a little drink, maybe a few pages of a new book and even a little snooze when the fancy takes you. I can guarantee that 99% of such passengers will choose to give you and your baby a wide berth, no matter how cute your bundle is and that means that your little one can now sleep or play on the extra seat you have bagged while you recline with a nice glass of wine.

Making Connections

After an uneventful flight, where Isabella slept and played happily in the middle seat, we arrived in Athens to hustle, bustle and a thrill in the air that made my spine tingle. We took the metro, which we quickly found doubled up as a great monkey-bar playground, into the centre to pick up our bus tickets, and enjoyed several hours soaking up the sun, people-watching in a local park. Isabella found it a great deal of fun crawling around on the grass, but it left me thinking, "How am I going to hand wash those grass stains out of the knees?" Ah well, there is no greater joy than seeing my daughter having fun and I have come to accept that fun to her usually equals messy.

The bus journey went without a hitch, not least because we managed to find the right bus stop. It was several years previously that we had last found ourselves in Athens and oh how I reminisce about those heady pre-baby days where we flounced around with just one small rucksack each, sipping beer and eating dolma in backstreet bars. Alas, it was not this that almost saw us miss our connection that time. We were standing at the wrong bus stop, and as buses to Aghios are few and far between, missing our connection would have meant an overnight stay and a whole host of other complications. In our defence there had been a demonstration and the street that ran past the travel agent was blocked, but we thought we had tracked down the bus stop where we should have been standing. However, about 10 minutes before our bus was due I started to realise that something must be wrong. All the other people waiting looked like office workers or locals and I thought it odd that on a bus that only had one stop, the port, nobody had luggage, just fancy clutch handbags. With minutes to spare we decided to run up the blocked street and see if there was somewhere else we should be. Thankfully, as we ran, we saw a rotund Greek woman with spiky red heels, red lipstick and a clipboard held high in the air marching down the street shouting in Greek as a gaggle of what looked to be tourists with large suitcases fell into a jumbled line behind her. We quickly established that she was leading them all to the bus and slipped in behind, following the click clack of her shoes - in which she expertly negotiated the cobbled streets.

On this, our family trip, there had been no fast-moving red shoes; our stop in Athens had been decidedly uneventful as well as relaxing and when we boarded, Isabella settled down pretty quickly on my lap and closed her eyes. This allowed me to take in silently the views of a city that merges from old to new with ease. Towering glass buildings interspersed with historic architecture, reflections and shadows casting themselves across parks where youngsters lounged on mopeds and older residents sat upright on wooden benches.

As I was losing myself in the streets my thoughts began to drift over the rooftops until quite suddenly, before I had really had chance to register, the fumes of the city were far behind and we were out on the open road; long expanses of tarmac stretched out ahead. To some it might be a relatively uninspiring journey to Aghios Constantinos, but to me it allowed me time to empty my mind and soak up this new country. Dusty, calm and dominated by a deep orange sky, as we left the city further and further behind the road began to run parallel with the blue waters. I felt strangely rested and became mesmerised as the waves curled and intertwined, enticing each other into the late afternoon sun.

Of course, it was too much to expect Isabella to sleep the entire journey and as we neared the end she woke up and became fractious. We tried plying her with toys, none of which stopped the tears, but thankfully a lovely Greek lady in front of us was more than happy to entertain her with a keyring, which kept Isabella smiling until it was taken away, at which point she let her disapproval be known quite vocally. She was an extremely determined child even then. But the great thing about the Greeks is that they LOVE children and are hugely accommodating to their presence in most situations, with or without tears, and the lady simply passed over the keyring, happy to see my daughter's eyes light up again.

> One thing I realised on this trip is that old toys will not hold Isabella's attention if she is in the mood to protest against her travelling life. I therefore now always have a handful of new items or toys she has never seen before, or that she sees as forbidden. I whip these out when the pressure gets too much to buy myself some peace.

The port of Aghios Constantinos itself is small and pretty and although there is not much going on, you could certainly while away an evening watching the sea lap against the shore and the sun go down. For us it was wait of only an hour or so, so we plonked ourselves down on plastic chairs, peeled off our sandals and indulged in an ice-cold beer. Isabella crawled around on the floor and then after discovering that the toilet at our chosen café was not really kitted out for baby changing, Scott managed to duck behind the bar to use a table under an awning.

> When you're travelling with your baby you cannot afford to be shy. If they need a bum change and there is no obvious place for this to happen, you must just get on with it and take care of things in the most comfortable place you can.

The time slipped away quite comfortably until we saw our boat trundling in from a distance and all around us we could feel and hear the stirring of passengers, uncurling their fingers from bottles, easing their feet slowly back into their shoes. By the time the whirring of the boat was close, we were all hovering with our luggage anticipating a silent evening cruise across calm waters to Skopelos once again.

Strangers On The Boat To Skopelos

Strangers on the boat were welcome because of course silence was the last thing on Isabella's mind, having forgone all routine to sleep pretty much throughout the rest of the day. I think it would be fair to say that she had reached breaking point and was letting us know the only way a baby can. Oh yes, she was screaming. Very loudly. Those high-pitched screams that make your ribcage rattle and your shoulders shudder. I know, there you were thinking that my daughter was perfect and did little more than sleep on practically every trip. Well, she is pretty good, but as she gets older it gets harder. Now there are only a few places that I like to be when my daughter has a serious tantrum and one of them just happens to be Greece. As I have said many times: Mediterranean cultures adore babies and if they cry – all the better! Because this gives complete strangers an excuse to relieve you of your child and gently calm them for you.

At first it can be unnerving sitting on a boat watching your one-year-old daughter being passed around cooing passengers and staff, both young and old. But once you slip out of the mode of thinking no-one is to be trusted and remember that you are now in Greece where freely fussing over children, throwing them up in the air and showering them with kisses is perfectly normal, then it becomes a magical experience. As we sat in our seats watching darkness descend on the waters Isabella was being looked after in the middle of the boat by an elderly Greek man travelling from Athens to spend the summer at his house on Alonissos as well as a young woman on vacation to visit her parents. Isabella stopped crying for a good amount of time and did not seem remotely phased by the fact that she was being chucked around by strangers. Of course, once she had enough she made it known, and she was passed back to us for cuddles, but having the united support of a whole boat is quite something.

> Travelling in Mediterranean countries with a baby is really quite something. You will quickly get used to walking into any shop, from the bakery to the supermarket, and being given free gifts for your little one. And when people reach out to take your baby, don't worry, it is perfectly normal for this to happen so sit back and enjoy a beer!

We eventually arrived in Skopelos late at night, jumped in a taxi and headed straight to our house and to bed. Although 18 hours travel by car, plane, train, bus and boat had been perfectly doable and, dare I say it, fairly enjoyable, we were too tired even to be tempted by a beer down at the Souvlaki.

Easter With Friends

If you visit Skopelos in April you see this part of the world in a completely different light. The island is peacefully stirring itself out of winter slumber, the grass a lush green; its parched summer blades nourished with rain. Wild flowers are in bloom and bright colours speckle every turn. As the soft scents of marjoram and pine reach your nostrils, you can't fail to lie back and relax. Of course it is also nice that there are very few tourists, the daytime weather is just warm enough for a T-shirt, but not unbearably hot, tavernas are quieter, leaving your children free to run around with the local kids or as often happens here, be looked after by the proprietor, you have the beaches to yourself, even if it's a little too cold to swim and most importantly you get to experience the true culture of traditional Greece.

And culture it was on this trip because when we finally arrived on Skopelos we were plunged straight into Easter week, apparent instantly due to the sound of ancient prayers sung by priests. Their voices travelled down from the church higher up the hill, coming to land in soft mesmerising echoes that bounced around our walls. This sound formed the most perfect of background noises as we ate leisurely lunches on our balcony and by the end of our stay we had begun to take these calming sounds resonating around our house for granted, but let's face it – lying in the bath listening to priests singing doesn't happen every day where I come from. It was a very special time of year to visit the island and although I am not particularly religious myself, the embrace of a community where religious traditions are valued is very seductive.

By way of integrating further, we decided to wander up the steep steps of the village, our feet dodging the crags and avoiding stone that would crumble beneath us, to join the rest of the residents who had been at the church for their celebration. Women whom you might normally see wandering around the streets or passing the time of day on their verandas dressed in house dresses and aprons, their hair hidden underneath headscarves, were out in their finery and men normally seen on their small tractors with flat caps, chewing on a matchstick, were suited and booted. We sat in the pretty courtyard of the local café drinking thick Greek coffee that stuck pleasantly to the roof of my mouth and watched the locals come and go, embracing and talking animatedly with visiting relatives. Isabella was passed round; at this stage she was only able to walk if someone held her hands so we watched as local children helped her stroll up and down the cobbled path next to raised white beds of colourful flowers. I thought to myself, there is nothing that makes me glow more than seeing my daughter exploring and learning from this vantage point.

As the crowds eventually started to disperse we wandered back in the late afternoon sun, and were collared halfway along by our neighbours who had travelled down from Thessaloniki the previous day to this, their inherited family home. Young, old, siblings, parents – a group of about seven were sitting outside, sharing some beautiful homemade dishes. Before we could even say *Yasas* chairs were hastily grabbed from inside and we were ushered into our seats and welcomed to eat with them. Dolma made with leaves from the Venetian ruin opposite, tzatziki and warm bread followed by fresh strawberries dipped in sugar and lashings of ouzo. Our neighbours spoke no English but with our smattering of Greek and a good dictionary we got by and soon realised that the language of football is universal. As Scott sat with the other menfolk, all slapping each other on the back as names of football teams, laughter and cigarette smoke escaped their mouths, I watched Isabella crawling around on the cobbled path, a healthy Greek woman pinching her cheeks and thought to myself how nice it is that at some points in life, very little is more than adequate.

We were only on the island for four days this time. As it was out of tourist season, many places were shut so most evenings were spent cooking, eating on our balcony and pondering the different lives of people all over the world.

Often we considered living in Glossa but ultimately although we felt the upbringing for Isabella would be free and easy, we didn't think it would provide her with enough other opportunities. But certainly we enjoyed allowing her to experience these places and hope to continue to do so. Many people have however made the leap from England to live on Skopelos - such as Roger & Jo Fox, who along with their Greek partner, Angelo, sell houses in Glossa. Roger had been on a boating holiday a few years before and spied Glossa from the port of Loutraki: "That's the kind of place I dream of living," he had remarked to the rest of his group before taking a slow amble up for a nose. Not long afterwards, he and his wife became the owners of a rundown place on the outskirts of the village and having edged themselves over slowly, both became permanent residents in 2007. Their business was set up so as to make it easier for foreigners to buy houses on the island because although it's fun to track down someone's brother's cousin via the Souvlaki and do deals in their mother's living room, it isn't necessarily the best way to do business for everyone. We had bumped into them over dinner that night and they filled us in about how the work was coming along on their holiday cottages, joking about how many empty Amstel bottles they had to clear out every day when the builders left. It's thirsty work, you know, and drinking on the job must work, because when we wandered with them to see how their latest rental cottage was coming along, we were dumbfounded.

Clifftop Cottage is perched on the very edge of the cliff and the sunset from its veranda, stretching over the water to the neighbouring island of Skiathos, takes your breath away. We sat for a while chatting then feeling a little squiffy after a few beers and armed with tips on where to visit in Athens, we strolled back to our part of the village and spent the following day preparing to leave on the next leg of our Greek travels.

Athens On A Budget

I had long dreamt of Athens; a place steeped in history, intrigue and mystery. This love of historical destinations probably started when I studied Humanities by correspondence course, initially because of my interest in art and philosophy yet surprisingly, it was our studies of the Roman Coliseum that held my attention most. I became fascinated with this iconic symbol of Rome and the history that runs through its now crumbling walls, and was thrilled to spend two romantic weeks in the city in 2002. Not with a man I hasten to add, but alone. I lost myself within its myriad cobbled alleyways, talking to street painters about the women of this vast and captivating city, sipping coffee in side-street cafes and admiring the Trevi fountain at dusk. My hope for Athens was that on this, my first lengthy visit, I would feel a similar sense of awe.

Due to our small budget and the fact that we had unwittingly stumbled into this city during Easter week, which meant most museums and even restaurants were either closed or running a slim service and many dwellers had departed for holidays on surrounding islands, we knew we would mostly be viewing the sights from afar and simply wandering. To some this might seem tedious, but to me drifting aimlessly along the many paths that a city has to offer makes me feel that I am getting to know a place intimately, not just popping in to see the sights that everyone says I should. I soak it up; smells, faces, colours, life, instead of just skimming over the surface or scooting round the periphery.

When I visited Copenhagen back in 2002 I walked down to see the statue of the Little Mermaid. The weather was crisp and cold, the blue sky occasionally clouding over with thick pockets of white that made me feel as if snow was imminent. I stared down at my purposefully striding black boots, the brisk air lighting up my face, making me smile. And when I reached her, I found a bench and sat for well over an hour wrapped up in my scarf and coat just staring, wondering, thinking and soaking up the atmosphere. As I did I observed with interest the numerous taxis that drove up and pulled over. In the space of a few seconds a tourist would jump out, a camera would click, then just as quick the order for the driver to depart, probably to the airport, would be given. I wondered what that picture would mean to them. How would they describe the place to their friends when they got back home? What would they know about this famous landmark? By taking the time to notice the seemingly inconsequential pieces of a place you are more likely to fall in love with it. I don't fall for obvious tokens of pleasure or appeal, but instead I seek out the hidden jewels of a place, looking at it from a different perspective. This means that my affair with a destination is hopefully passed on to others with colourful words that brim with excitement.

In Athens these jewels were in abundance: the smell of local food drifting through the air from dark doorways, weathered faces sharing beer, young couples leaning into each other over coffee, street entertainers and market traders beckoning and of course not forgetting the dog that navigated the city streets astride the roof of his owner's car. I responded to the city just as I have to others, but it was different to the original comparisons I had made to Rome. There is less glamour, less pretence and more of the earthy grit of real life. With this comes comfort and a relaxed experience and although I'm sure we could have got away with taking Isabella to a museum for an hour or two if we timed it over her nap, it was nice to dawdle through the quiet streets and let her soak things up from the buggy. I actually now believe that this could quite easily have been the best time to visit with Isabella. Maybe if the crowds had been bulging off the pathways, she might have been more restless, we would have felt under pressure and our pace would have had to be faster and less leisurely.

> We were lucky to stumble on a quiet Athens during Easter week. This is a useful lesson: it would be wise to visit a city with a little one at a quieter time. It is less overwhelming for little eyes and ears and everyone has a more enjoyable experience.

We headed off at a gentle pace, planning our route on foot. Beneath the Acropolis we wandered taking pictures, strolling up back alleys where cats rested under the fuchsia pink bougainvilleas that bordered black iron gates recessed into white-washed walls. We viewed the Agora from afar and figured that this was as good as viewing it close up and Isabella was fascinated by the Evzone pom-pomguards at Syntagma Square and was happy to stroll freely around the many secret paths found in the National Gardens, as well as enjoying the mini zoo. And when we stopped in lively *Plaka* for beer and sandwiches she crawled around under the tables charming the proprietor, an elderly man who looked like he had seen a fair few things in his time. The added bonus to our trip was that several times we accidentally stumbled on various religious celebrations and managed to sidle our way into the crowds to observe priests in all their splendour, submersing ourselves in their harmonious voices and relishing in the fact that we were seeing Athens somewhat as a local, not just as a tourist.

When visiting a city do ensure you include a healthy choice of activities to keep your baby happy. We allowed Isabella to run free in the park in between doing the things we wanted to do and we found that small, relaxed cafes were a much better option than sitting down to a fancy lunch in a posh restaurant.

SIX

Open-Ended Family Travel

Taking To The Roads of Europe

Before and during Isabella's first year our home stood amidst the busy roads, vast shopping centre and walkways of a small city and when we lived there one of our favourite things to do was stop for a tapas lunch in a local Spanish restaurant. We enjoyed sharing paella in surroundings lit by soft candles melting into old wine bottles, where traditional Spanish music drifted in to permeate our conversations. Our small table in the dark and cosy corner of this restaurant felt miles away from everyday city living. It was therefore fitting that on a rather unremarkable day in 2006, while I was carrying our daughter in the womb, this was the place we planned a new direction for our life.

I wouldn't say we didn't like our life, in fact quite the opposite. We had a comfortable house on a quaint estate that we were rather fond of, a multitude of walks for us and our dog close by, Scott had a reasonably secure job and I was over the moon at being able to work from an office in our garden. With the impending arrival of our baby this setup would allow me to fulfil my desire to be a stay-at-home mum, bringing in money as well as pursuing my dreams. Life was pretty peachy really. But as we shared our tapas we discussed the fact that life, although peachy, was pretty predictable and the prospect that our itchy feet would be scratched only by short breaks and annual holidays did not reassure our travelling spirits. Our personal belief is that you only get one shot at life and whoever imposed a rule that said you must do the same thing throughout it? Nobody actually, but we had certainly fallen into a routine that was comfortable, but, which did not particularly enrich us and certainly was not one we wanted to stay in forever. And thus we decided to throw our hands up in the air in defiance and say what the hell, let's do something crazy and the decision to take a long-term road trip as a family was born out of a longing to travel for travel's sake, but also from a desire to spend some precious time with our, as yet, unborn child and possibly, potentially, change our lifestyle in the long-term.

Of course, talking about it over a glass of sangria is one thing, putting these hare-brained schemes into action is a whole new ballgame and it's much easier to say, "Oh, let's just dial a pizza, put the TV on and forget about it." But, as people who know us know; if we get an idea in our heads, no matter how seemingly crazy it sounds, the likelihood is that we will go on to put it into action. When I worked as a copywriter back in 2005 Scott and I took a holiday from work to spend a wonderful week on the Greek island of Alonissos. We zipped about on our moped, supped cocktails in hilltop bars and generally fell in love with the idea of living part of the year in such a place. I would say "I'm going to be a writer and this could be my creative escape for six months of the year," and Scott would say, "Yeah and I will get to do up an old house and chop wood and we can just hide away every winter." I always remember returning to work and announcing that this was what we intended to do and several colleagues remarking, "Oh Alice, everyone who goes on holiday comes back and says that". But do it we did, well half of it anyway. We bought the old house, did it up and loved it, and although since then our family circumstances have changed and we have chosen to sell it instead of spending six months of every year there, we can still put it down to experience. I guess I can rest easy knowing that I will never have to wonder what might have happened if we had gone ahead and bought a retreat in Greece, because now I know.

And that's pretty much how we live our life. Think it – do it, and don't worry about the outcome because whatever that is, it will always lead onto something else. So when we discussed the option of selling up and travelling Europe in a camper, we knew it would happen; it was just a matter of sorting out the logistics. We wanted to make sure that we were all ready to make the trip by settling into parenthood and enjoying some family holidays in our baby's first year. Then we needed to sell our house in a market that appeared to be on the downturn, save some money and lastly find and buy a suitable camper that was up to taking us all around Europe indefinitely. We therefore aimed for a leaving date not long after our unborn baby's first birthday and to get the ball rolling, six weeks after Isabella was born, we put the house on the market… and waited.

When we made the decision to leave our life behind and head off on a travelling adventure, we decided to wait until Isabella was a year old. At this point she had had most of her early immunisations and we had also managed to get a few trips in to check that we were all up for it on a longer-term basis.

Life As We Know It Is Over

Our plan had been that the house would go on the market and in the current climate it would take up to a year to sell. If it miraculously sold quickly, we could rent a house for six months for what remained of the time before the big departure. But, dear reader, how the best-laid plans sometimes do backflips and pull funny faces at you as they land. The first potential buyers arrived to view our home within a week: a confident and brash couple who jumped up and down on the floorboards to see if they were solid, and opened all my kitchen cupboards for a nose inside. They talked about where their cars could go, where the rabbit hutches might live, what they were going to use my beloved garden office for – a utility room - ooo, the shame! - and even the wall their flat screen TV would hang on. It all seemed so rushed and mechanical, lacking the compassion I felt our home deserved and I couldn't help but think that they would not fit in to our quiet cul-de-sac, or that our house would embrace them warmly. However, they offered the asking price and with a sense of foreboding, we accepted and started packing. Here I was with a daughter less than two months old, only just starting to get to grips with motherhood and suddenly I was beginning a journey towards homelessness and the unknown, yet I felt strangely elated at the prospect of our adventure. But no sooner had we piled all our boxes high and packed away things that were not essential to the everyday running of our life, they pulled out.

> I wish I could give you a top tip about the best time to leave behind your life to enter into open-ended travel, but I can't. There really is no good time to take such a big jump – you simply have to remind yourself of the dreams you have and work towards them matter-of-factly. The one thing you need to worry least about, though, is your child. If they are young, they will surprise you with their nonchalant attitude towards new routines and new surroundings. Of course, if you are in a position to rent your property out to go travelling then I believe this would be an ideal scenario.

Months of gut-wrenching sales and no-sales followed, but somewhere in between we managed to get married with family and friends by our side in Greece, watch Isabella's first roll, first crawl, listen to her first word and take all of the trips I have talked about in this book so far. We had also left our belongings packed up and ready for a departure that we were not entirely sure would ever happen, since the first viewers had pulled out, but somehow, amidst the mayhem, we retained a sense of humour and kept our life and our home content and happy. Two weeks before Isabella's first birthday we moved out of our beloved home and as I walked around the empty house, touching each surface, closing my eyes and smelling the air, remembering everything that had happened within those walls, I felt a twinge of sadness.

That house had played a huge part in my life. It was the first place I had lived as an adult and felt my restless soul calmed, for a while anyway. Never before had I expected to fall in love with a man and feel so content, and much of the nurturing of my marriage had happened within that unassuming exterior. I had very nearly given birth to my daughter there on a crisp sunny March day and we held our previous dog, Levi, in our arms as she took her last breaths, before burying her underneath the Christmas tree in the garden. To me a house is far more than bricks and mortar. Memories run through the walls, entwine themselves around the beams; pieces of ourselves are woven into the fabric and as I shut that door, I took a deep breath and hoped that we were not as crazy as some people said we were.

Our New Camper Home

When I was about eight years old we moved from the North of England to the South and I had (how should I put it?), a distinguished accent. Like most eight-year-olds I desperately wanted to fit in and so when we moved to a city estate into a standard cul-de-sac I thought that if I didn't sound like everyone else then at the very least I wanted our house to look like everyone else's with, you know, maybe a car that didn't stand out from all the Cavaliers and Escorts. But no, my family has always been slightly different. We never did normal, and instead of a pillar-box red garage door, we had peaches and cream and instead of a beige Rover, we had a day-glo orange VW Beetle. I'll never forget the day my dad brought this peculiar addition back to the family home. There I was hanging out in the street in my roller skates trying to be cool when my dad pulled round the corner tooting the horn with one hand and waving like the Queen with the other. I just rolled my eyes and thought, "Why can't we just be like everyone else?" When you're eight you haven't yet realised the benefit of being a little quirky and I'm sure that it is precisely due to this background that I'm not afraid to go out on a limb. And for that I am now thankful, because when it came to our new home, fear of being different just would not have cut it.

We had bought it before moving out of our house and much as I had dreams of cruising down dusty dirt tracks in a split screen camper, sadly with our family situation and for the length of time we were intending to spend away, that idea had long been shelved. No, instead we opted for a folding camper; not a caravan, because that seemed too fuddy duddy, but a camper that folded out into something that did in fact resemble a caravan. Very much. But it was still technically a camper and that fitted with my – trying to be a little cool – self and as our folding camper was officially called a Dandy Destiny, we thought it was rather fitting for our adventure. We bought it from a lovely couple who had it from new 15 years previous and were clearly very attached to it. As we drove it away we almost had to make an emergency stop to free ourselves of them as they clung to the back…15 years of family holidays were inside that trailer; It was literally a box full of memories. But knowing that we were planning on filling it with even more, hopefully good ones, they eventually let go.

> We would have loved to travel in a VW camper, but with a baby and a dog, this just would not have been practical. If you're planning on doing a similar trip; short or long-term, do consider how much space you need to move around, change your baby's bum, as well as having a little of your own space when your child goes to bed.

Our memories did not however start in the rolling hills of SW France or even on the pebbly south coast of England. No, instead our new abode was parked on Scott's parents' drive for three long months because the time between moving out of our house and departing was too short to take on a rental lease. This turned out to be a good thing, because living on their drive it gave us the opportunity to get used to camper living, with mod cons on hand should we need them. You see, the reality about life in our camper was that we had no toilet and no running water and waking up in the freezing English winter nights to head out in the dark for the loo, although not the most pleasant thing in the world, was better than not having one at all. We needed to ease ourselves in slowly. I suppose that looking back it does seem more crazy than it did at the time because when you are fulfilling a dream you have to remain so focused within it that there is no room to doubt what you are doing. Strangely, Isabella was comfortable, her sleeping pattern unchanged and her reaction to this new life relaxed. This made us feel comfortable, too. In the morning she enjoyed racing up and down the camper over and over and jumping all over the bed with its huge cushions, and when it was cooking time she was happy to sit in her Bumbo at the table, playing with her puzzles and books while eating little bits of whatever we were making.

> One of the best items we took away with us in our camper was the Bumbo – a kind of little seat that sits quite steadily on most surfaces and keeps your baby in a good sitting position. When my oldest and dearest friend gave it to us as a present I didn't really understand it, but it has proved invaluable in so many situations and was the perfect height for our Dandy table.

Of course, the best thing about living in a folding camper in addition to it being dry and cosy, was that sleeping with just a thin piece of material between us and the open sky gave our souls a sense of freedom, even when it was just in the back garden. We would wake up to the sounds of trees rustling, wind howling and we liked being able to tell what the weather was like without even having to peer out of our window. We started to wonder why we had ever lived in a house at all.

Everyday Life In A Small Space

Life in a small space was certainly interesting especially as, for some of the time at least, we were living in our home on wheels in England during the depths of a British winter. Inside our four plastic walls we made hot soups, wrapped up in shawls and extra blankets at night, lit candles and read books and lived a peaceful and quiet existence. It was, ultimately, a pretty romantic and enriching experience free of modern trappings. We savoured how our senses were heightened, how we became more aware of small things. During this time I thought a lot about my parents and how they had lived in a caravan for many years as newlyweds and with three of their children. I felt as though we were almost reliving a part of their life, experiencing in real time the stories I had grown up with: how they would put the kids to bed, make their bed up and sit listening to the wireless, playing cards together. I developed a newfound admiration for my mother's ability to make a home within that space for her husband and children.

The thing about small babies and children is that if you get them used to things young, you stand a good chance of them being quite amenable when it comes to fitting in when you need them to. Isabella got used to sleeping in her own curtained area of the camper pretty quickly with neither party causing much disturbance for the other. I'm not sure I would want to do this after the age of two, but when she was a baby it was fine.

The truth is that I think if we had three children in our camper the romantic picture would have become a little worn around the edges pretty quickly. However, with one it really was no problem, despite how people looked at me when I said this. You see one of the most asked questions during that time was how we managed to live in a camper with a one-year-old and a dog. People could not believe that this could be fun, but for us it was. When we laid Isabella in her cot and closed the dark curtains, she would drift off to sleep as normal. We could talk, watch movies and go about our life without fear of waking her and I could even get away with running the sewing machine. In the mornings it was a little more tricky but the beauty of Isabella being less than a year old meant that I could pop her in her cot to play with toys or read a book as I busied myself demisting, airing out and rearranging our camper into day mode. Certain tasks had to be done, regularly each day. I think had I paused my daily routine, everyday camper living might have become nightmarish and been cited as the main culprit in an eventual divorce.

The most important thing to remember about small space living is that everything takes longer within the confines of 14ft by 7ft. Getting a pan out to make dinner, for instance, meant taking all the cupboard contents out before replacing them piece–by-piece to fit them back in again, although it didn't put us off our cooking. We produced all manner of wonderful meals with the two rings, a small grill and our limited array of utensils, but we did treat ourselves to Sunday lunch at the pub once a week. "I can't believe we used to moan about our kitchen being small! Now we are living in a home that could fit inside it," I would say to Scott, and we would laugh. Which is just as well because there were no rooms to run to after an argument and pulling curtains does not have the same effect as slamming a door. Instead, for three months we did our best to continue our normal life, with Scott going to work every day and me running my home business via a satellite and the Internet café. When we became frustrated we would focus on our goal: a road trip with no known end and a feeling of freedom little known by most young families. Yes, we were stepping outside our comfort zone, but it made us feel alive, as if we were somehow truly living by taking a chance.

Preparing For Our Departure

Marie-Françoise threw her hands around the air, her animated voice directed at Scott, "No, no, no, you are not English! The way you talk! The way you move your arms! No, no, no, you are most definitely not English! Check your family tree!" In the opinion of our French teacher, it seems that my husband is not the humble Luton boy we thought he was but in fact a passionate Mediterranean and during lessons over coffee as Isabella enjoyed her midday nap, we both hoped that this was a positive sign that at least one of us might be able to pick up this new and beautiful language easily.

Marie-Françoise had been coming to our house once a week since our plan had first been hatched because, for us, it was important to learn a language and as we felt particularly drawn to France, it seemed as good a place as any to start. She had moved to England many years previous and we so looked forward to our lessons where she would waft in with co-ordinated accessories and an air of French chic. She was always confident in our abilities and basking in her praise of our commitment, we looked forward to these lessons with enthusiasm but we had, for some time, refrained from sharing all our plan with Marie-Françoise. I'm not entirely sure why but I guess that announcing to someone that you plan to move into a folding camper on your parents' drive for three months prior to the big departure sounded a little odd, even to us, so instead we told her we weren't sure what we would do in between leaving our house and leaving for France. Of course, we needn't have worried. Our eventual request that she continue to teach us in our home on wheels was met with big smiles and on her first visit to our new abode, as I invited her to take a seat under the tight-fitting camping table before - in a much more unsophisticated manner - I squeezed myself under, she looked around her eyes filled with enthusiasm and announced, "Ahhh, I lurve itttt". And when Isabella awoke from behind the curtain and sat alongside us as we learned, Marie-Françoise endeared herself to our family even further. It was with much sadness that we approached the end of our cosy camper lessons, but we were now at least armed with some language skills that might get us through any sticky moments during the first leg of our family travels through France.

> Not only will learning at least some of a language aid you in any complicated situations, you will find that as it is likely your baby will be mixing with local children, knowing enough to make small talk with their parents will come in very handy.

Those last few days of life as we knew it are a blur, lost in a haze that clouds over a part of my life that now seems very long ago. We ran around busily buying computer leads, plastic dinner sets, organising paperwork and squeezing in last-minute family visits. We suffered from emotions that ranged from exhaustion and feeling overwhelmed, to elation and enthusiasm. But never did we feel that we were not doing the right thing. Instead we found that in our own rare quiet moments it took all our strength to hold back the excitement that came with the knowledge that soon we would be heading into the unknown, our only security each other and the home we had tied to the back of our truck.

SEVEN

Let The Road Trip Begin

Call Of The Road

When people say there are no words to describe a feeling or situation I wonder what it is that can make an emotion so strong, so consuming that you simply cannot express yourself. For me words to convey how it felt the day we drove away from our life that escape me, but I will do my best to at least describe the physical feeling. Our bodies felt alive with frequent jolts as if electricity was coursing through our veins. Our minds were free and empty; it was as if our thoughts had escaped and were dancing around the car merging together to make one big magical force. Maybe you could liken it to the moment you know you've found love and it is reciprocated, or when your new baby is placed in your arms. Or quite possibly it was a similar feeling to the euphoria experienced when you tell your egotistical and derogatory boss to stuff their job, and for a few delicious moments you feel on top of the world – à la Bridget Jones. We all had broad smiles on our faces and as Isabella and Milla gazed out of the window I glanced at Scott, touched his hand and we smiled a wide warm smile of contentment. For the first time a true sense of all we had dreamed was starting to feel real and we were free - from obligations, from time constraints, and free to just be a family. The hardest part had been selling and leaving our house and we had worked through all the emotions related to that, months earlier. No, we were happy to be going, didn't care when we would be back, and were filled with wonder about our impending adventure, secretly hoping that something might happen to change our lives forever. Right then, forever was a long way off, but that didn't stop us talking about it. You see, on the road you always have plenty of time. Time to soak up the scenery, to think and talk about all your hopes, dreams and desires.

> If you are thinking of a long-term road trip, do consider it when your baby is young and at their most transportable as this means minimal (I didn't say no) tantrums and grumps at being cooped up in the car for a few hours at a time.

We left Calais with whoops and cheers, remembering to drive on the right and stopping for our first croissants and French words not far from the port. Out of the window we watched the early morning sun lift itself slowly above the golden fields, whooped some more and then drove towards the Champagne region, a fitting destination to toast the start of our new life on the road.

First Stop Champagne

We had already booked our first campsite, although we did not plan to keep doing this. We wanted to experience life on the road and embrace not having somewhere to call home and although the thought of not knowing where we were going to sleep at night was marginally scary at times, it was also exhilarating. However, on our first trip with a young baby we didn't relish the thought of stumbling around in the dark, tired, bewildered and lost. Back in England we had scoured our camping book and picked out an idyllic looking site nestled amidst the peaceful rolling rapeseed fields of Thonnance les Moulins. Within minutes of arriving we were not sure whether this had been good or a bad choice. Good because the site was well-equipped, beautifully kept and extremely child-friendly, bad because it set a very high benchmark from which to compare all future overnight stops. Think 5* luxury all-inclusive hotel, just with tents – or campers – for accommodation. It was so lovely that for almost a week we were unable to drag ourselves away and head into the more rugged travelling adventure we had planned, feeling contented within the bosom of such luxury. "If I had known camping was this fantastic I would have moved out of my house a long time ago!" I jested to Scott as we supped cold beer and watched Isabella play. She was happy to splash for hours in her paddling pool on our huge grassy pitch, I had wireless Internet access and was able easily to keep my little bits of work going, so it seemed like the perfect place to digest the madness of the previous few weeks and settle into our new life on the road. Thinking back I imagine had we headed straight to a less salubrious campsite we might have been running back to our old life faster than our tent pegs could follow.

> A top-notch campsite really is an experience with something for all the family; so whether you are just planning a French camping getaway, or you too are venturing on the road long-term, I would highly recommend indulging in a bit of camping luxury for the first few nights. Believe you me – not all campsites are quite so well-appointed.

And so we sunbathed, took Isabella to the park and watched her play in the sand while we rested our heads against the wooden fence and picked grass; twisting it around our fingers, talking about whether a campsite might one day be a viable family business. We even talked to the owners – an English woman and her Dutch husband – about how they had ended up living this life. It turned out that they too had wanted a different kind of lifestyle, and had made the decision to sell up and meet somewhere in the middle of the Netherlands and England. We felt inspired and filled with optimism and the massive intakes of fresh country air that were filling our lungs helped to clear out the cobwebs, rejuvenating our minds. We hiked for hours through tiny villages whose cows looked at us nonchalantly and farmer's wives eyed us suspiciously from doorways, sleepy toddlers slung idly on their hips. Packed lunches and coffee were enthusiastically consumed on creaky logs in shadowy forests and I would bend down and pick flowers with my daughter and think 'this is what life is about'.

> When our daughter was born we were lucky enough to be passed down some wonderful items, one of which was a backpack. The backpack became indispensable from about the age of eight months and can be used up to the age of three. It's perfect if you are into walking or navigating your way through the cobbled and steep alleyways of traditional French towns!

Of course, if only it was always so romantic, which sadly it was not in my daughter's eyes. The one thing we hadn't planned for was how it would feel to live our everyday life in the constant presence of others, which is what happens on a campsite. Yes you can look for a pitch further away, but it is not always guaranteed that you might not return to your camper to be faced with a topless couple sunbathing directly opposite. We have usually been fairly lucky in finding a quiet space, but there have been occasions when we have found ourselves surrounded and on this particular campsite, due to its high-star rating and thus popularity, we did have a number of fellow campers nearby. Prying eyes were not much of a problem because high bushes surrounded us, but sound-wise it was not the best. In a terraced house you can hear neighbours going about their business through the wall, so you can imagine what it is like when there is only material separating one pitch from the next. And the sounds that were emanating from our abode at this point were those of our young daughter screaming because she didn't want to go to bed or she wanted the bottle that we were trying to wean her off.

What we realised quickly is that everyone else is on holiday while we were still trying to live our everyday existence, albeit in a more leisurely way. But, the fact that we were travelling long-term and thus trying to retain some sort of routine was of course of no interest to other campers. Picture the scene: a warm summer's dusk, birds chirping softly in the trees, a nearby stream's waters bubbling by in the distance, in your hand a glass of chilled white wine and your husband, boyfriend, partner or lover is to your left. You're talking about life and what you want to do; making plans for the future and you've got that warm, fuzzy, floaty holiday feeling. But, oops – hold that thought, because right at this fuzzy moment you need to add a baby screaming at the top of her lungs in the next pitch then, as you look over, you will see us; harassed and guilty parents because all that is shielding our daughter's screams from you relaxed holiday makers is one thin layer of material. On a normal holiday we would have thrown caution to the winds and let her run around until she fell asleep in a crumpled heap on our laps wrapped up in a blanket and bathed in soft candlelight. But after a few nights of this we were fed up of having to deal with the aftermath: a grumpy and tired Isabella. So we came to the conclusion that routine is vital even on the road. So, we learned to grow a thick skin quickly and face our disapproving neighbours – who shot us frequent looks at the washing-up sinks and injected yawns into morning conversations – with laughter and apologies. Yes, it can be embarrassing, but you do get over it.

> **When your baby insists on keeping fellow campers up all night the best way to deal with the fallout is to face it head-on. Smile and apologise and you'll find that bar a few, most will be understanding. Who knows what they're saying when they turn away. But who cares?!**

After a relaxing week in camper luxury, we decided we had inflicted enough pain on others, and decided it was time to truly let our road trip begin. The Champagne region had been good to us, a fitting start to our adventure, feeding our minds with fresh air and igniting our imagination as we held our faces into the sun and felt her ground crackle and crunch beneath our walking boots; but we were ready to see more of the world around us.

In-Car Entertainment

Morning dew was on the ground, glistening between my toes; the predicted rain was still not overshadowing the morning sun that seemed brighter reflecting off the rapeseed fields. It had taken a while to psyche ourselves up, but now we were itching to get going. So, slippery under sandals we pushed, pulled, fell over and let out a few expletives until eventually Dandy was securely hitched to the back of the wagon. The strangest thing about this scenario was the absence of that deflated 'got to get all the way back home now' feeling, imagining instead the long drive ahead and wondering where we were going to stay that night. By the time we got in the car, we wondered why it had taken us so long to get back on the open road.

With time on our side we avoided the toll roads in favour of driving through quaint villages and towns. In particular the drive through the walled town of Langres was interesting and it was nice to pass briefly through Dijon and see all the sights; beautiful houses on hillsides and students hanging out around town smoking cigarettes. The other side of Dijon led into spectacular countryside and we wondered if every new place we would go would be better than the last. The loose plan was to head towards a small village in Burgundy region where Scott's dad owns some land, and we anticipated that this was a good five-hour drive. At this point we had not yet perfected the art of keeping young children entertained which as passenger, generally fell to me, because up until this trip Isabella had been very small and preferred to doze for long periods during car journeys. Now, at a year old, she was well aware when it was playtime, lunchtime, sleep time and even in the car carried out these daily activities accordingly. Let's just say I was up to speed fairly quickly.

> When you're heading off on a long car journey make sure you have a good selection of stories and children's nursery rhymes on CD. They can be a godsend when nothing else will do and mesmerised my daughter.

In my opinion, unless you're happy to put your child in front of a DVD for the entire journey, you need to think creatively and thus 'this little piggy' in rap, operatic, and country style rolled off my tongue with ease by the end of the journey because although Isabella was happy to look out of the window for a couple of hours, after that it was time to move the entertainment up a notch. CDs, from Pooh Bear to nursery rhymes, were a godsend – but only if I mimed or did funny actions along with them and after a while she decided that she was up for a bit of a boogie so at this point I managed to slip in some Oasis, Prince and Madonna to keep the adults happy, too. When we stopped for a roadside lunch I decided to swap places with Milla and sit in the back so that I could do some colouring with Isabella, read her stories and get her settled for a doze. All lovely, but it was after the doze when she got that look on her face that said: "OK guys, I've been good as gold and hardly moaned a smidgen, but now I want to get out and no amount of you telling me it's only another five minutes is going to wash". We now discovered the joy of a glovebox road map – another 45 minutes' occupation.

Between the music, nursery rhymes and some of my bad singing with actions we all travelled comfortably, although I'm sure Scott would quite happily have booted me and my rapping out of the window.

> Always carry a few emergency toys in the car, toys your baby doesn't get to see or play with very often. Try adult items you're not worried about such as a glovebox map or pick up a few of the plentiful €1 toys on offer in newsagents and whip them out at difficult moments.

I looked at my reflection in the wing mirror, Milla's head sticking out of the window, her ears blowing in the wind and I thought to myself 'yes, this is the start of a very long and happy family road trip.'

Looking For The Sunshine

We rolled into Étang-sur-Arroux at the end of a long day, but it was still light and we were lucky enough to stumble upon a campsite just out of the town, 20 minutes away from where we wanted to be. Granted, it was basic to say the least – the complete opposite of our last stop - but it had everything we needed. We parked up in the middle of a field with cows opposite us, overlooking a river. For all the site lacked in services and tidiness it made up for in views and peace. The heavy air threatened rain, so we decided not to dilly dally and put the camper up straight away. But at that point no rain came so knowing we wanted to put the awning up too, but figuring that we had a little more time, we opted for a glass of wine in the last of the sun. Of course, no sooner had we parked our bums on our seats and laid out Isabella's blanket in the long grass, the black clouds started to roll in and within the hour we were battling wind and rain; our heavy awning flapping about. I was trying to hold the thing down with my legs, arms and mouth while Scott tried to peg it down without a mallet. The whole time I kept thinking how my dad would be so disappointed at our lack of organisation, but using the quick-thinking skills my parents gave me I produced a can of butter beans, which worked a treat and we managed to get finished just before the heavens did their worst. Of course, throughout the entire drama Isabella was happily playing in her travel cot in the warmth of the Dandy and Scott joked, "When she gets a bit older, there'll be no skiving off; she'll be able to help us instead of getting away with lounging around." Too true, life on the road does not allow for ladies of leisure.

> A traditional travel cot is a must when you're on the road, certainly up to the age of about 18 months. Not only is it the perfect sleeping place (we had ours on top of the camper bed!) but when you are busy putting up your tent or setting out your camper, you will be glad of somewhere to put your baby safely.

The next day the showers stuck around but unperturbed we headed into Autun for the day. We fell in love with this city steeped in Roman history, complete with a spectacular gothic spire standing proud against the Morvan hills. The lower parts are fairly modern with bowling alleys, McDonalds and lots of students milling around, but strolling further in to its heart we were soon wandering through winding streets lined with old houses, quaint shops, cafes and restaurants before we reached the rather impressive cathedral. Isabella was perfectly happy in her buggy throughout, not least because we stopped at a *pâtisserie artisan* for a treat, which we enjoyed on the bench of a cobbled street. The following day we had coffee with Scott's dad's French friends, and their parents all of who welcomed us into their home with enthusiasm and kindness. Afterwards we headed off to picnic deep in the forest-clad hills of Parc Régional du Morvan, the perfect place to ponder where the road would guide us next. As we looked up and saw more grey skies looming, heading South seemed the only logical direction.

Although at the beginning of our travels we chose to stay on campsites, over time we have realised how easily you can stay in places for free. Camping *libre* is allowed all over France – just ask before you pitch your tent! And designated picnic areas can be found throughout Europe, usually with water and loos provided. Obviously, if you have a camper/caravan with a toilet/shower inside you will be able to rough it quite comfortably for longer!

EIGHT

The South of France

The Kindness Of Strangers

"Let's go for broke and head South through the night," Scott announced. Fantastic, I thought. Driving south, direction Provence - how could I resist? Getting our heads around the fact that we had no plan and could do whatever we chose took a little time, but we had to get used to it, so as I pushed a lock of hair from Isabella's face to behind her ear I replied with a casual shrug and a glint in my eye, "OK, shall we leave now?"

By 4pm we were packed and on the road thinking that with a couple of stops we would be there by the early hours, at which point we would get a few zzzzs in the car before finding somewhere more permanent to rest. The first leg would take us to St Etienne and as it was still light we were hoping for some beautiful scenery. But as we got further away from Autun, it seemed we left the splendour of Burgundy behind us. However, the bouts of rain, fantastic cloud formations and spectacular rainbows made up for what the villages en route lacked in architectural splendour. The name St Etienne sounds more romantic than the place which is a bizarre mixture of industrial landscape, complete with ugly and invasive blocks of flats, set rather oddly within rolling hills; cows happily munching their way around the outside. For art-lovers there are some fantastic museums well worth a detour for in the recently rejuvenated centre, I believe. Other than that, driving through did not capture my imagination but as we drove away the scenery became more impressive. We entered the hills towards Annonay at dusk via narrow winding roads etched into dramatic rock-faces, but they were proving a strain for our load. The last note I made in my notebook that night was, "Will the Dandy make it?" I often tell Scott off for openly tempting fate, but I fear that night, it was entirely my doing.

Somewhere up said hillside we stopped for what we thought would be a leisurely sandwich in the car. I climbed out and instantly took a few snaps of the rock faces while Scott stretched his legs. Then all I remember hearing is, "What the hell is that?" I turned to see water pouring from underneath the bonnet down the hill. We stared at each other with our jaws on the floor. I gauge situations like this by checking with Scott, and as he had turned as white as a sheet, it confirmed that we were in trouble. We cheered up slightly when we found it wasn't the radiator but instead the overflow pipe that was leaking buckets of water, but we were still in a predicament. We had the choice of chugging uphill and blowing the engine, or rolling down, hoping we could get back to St Etienne to find a garage (on a Saturday night?) and book into a hotel. All I could think to say was that we should get back in the car to avoid the huge black clouds forming above us and try to get our heads around the situation. I had a heavy feeling in the pit of my stomach and both our expressions were dismal. We were horrified so soon into the trip to be faced with the possibility of such a nightmare car situation which probably could result in huge expense... So I can hardly express my joy when a battered old Peugeot 106 pulled up alongside us with a jolly-looking Frenchman inside sticking his thumb up at me to see if we were OK or not. Scott stepped out of the car with an exaggeratedly sad expression and the guy said, *"Je suis mécanicien"*. Oh thank you Lord, in our hour of need! Entirely in French - thanks to our lessons with Marie-Francoise - we explained the problem as best we could and he took over.

> During unexpected and extended periods of potential boredom for children in the car I can suggest rolling down the window and letting a funny French mechanic pull faces at them.

He had his full kit on board and after a bit of umming, ahhing, pushing and prodding he explained that the problem was something to do with things being blocked causing the thermostat to stop working. He told us to get back in the car for five minutes to let the engine cool, which we did. At this point the heavens opened and as we sat in the car we thought that this man was surely pulling our leg and would now drive off home to his wife, beer and a Saturday night DVD. But oh no, he promptly got out of his car wearing his mac, opened his boot, shone his torch under the bonnet and proceeded to take a bit out of our car, seal it up, reattach two other bits, put some special fluid in and hey presto, we were back in business. We of course had to be entirely trusting that he was *un vrai mecanicien* and attempted to note down *très* important information in French referring to the new part we needed. He assured us we would now be fine to happily get to Provence, and beyond. To be extra sure he said he would follow us up through the hills before taking the turn to his village, which he did before waving us a cheery good-bye. I wanted so much to express how grateful we were that he stopped on his way home, on a Saturday night, in the pouring rain, to help two English strangers, just because he could, but all I could manage to stutter out was, *"Vous êtes notre sauveur"*. To which he smiled and in his best English replied, *"Thank you very much Mr & Mrs. My pleasure"*. We tentatively trundled on, Isabella fast asleep and oblivious to most of the drama and we reached Orange in the early hours, where we slept in the car... and yes, it did feel romantic to wake up in Provence.

City Camping

After a surprisingly comfortable and extremely welcome few hours' sleep I climbed out at first light to stretch my arms, body and mind into the morning and get warm. I could see the sun starting to rise up behind the dark trees, its glaring strength almost blinding me. I grabbed the camera: I like to take pictures of specific moments to remember them later. As I turned back I saw a sleepy Isabella perched on the back of the truck in her pyjamas, clutching her favourite soft toy as always. Her eyes wide, but sleepy, she held on to Daddy for a morning cuddle. I framed them for my memory. I felt warm, encouraged and not the least bit worried about the car possibly being kaput. I was delighted to be living in a wagon with all that was precious to me at my fingertips.

> For me, undoubtedly the hugest benefit of longer-term travel when your children/child is small is the quality time you are able to spend together as a family. School and independence come far too quickly and our travelling life in Isabella's early years, I hope, will create a lasting bond.

Taking our roadside mechanic's word for it that our car would be fine for a few days – if not weeks – we decided not to head instantly to a garage, but instead to seize the glorious day and go in search of a campsite within the great expanses of vineyards and Cypress trees whose dark elongated shadows we had spied during our night drive. We trailed for hours through the most beautiful countryside dotted with rickety terracotta tiled houses with a distinct Tuscan feel; much-needed sun beating down on us. Eventually we stumbled upon a sign that took us so far up a mountainside we were surprised the car and camper made it, especially after our last hillside adventure, yet sadly, for all the engine's huffing and puffing, it was in vain. The campsite was not what we were looking for, the pitches tiny with no privacy, so we made fumbled apologies and headed back downhill. Quite randomly we had a new idea and decided that we would instead opt for a campsite within a city, well, almost.

Avignon, for centuries one of the artistic centres of France with its famous bridge and other fantastic sights, has a municipal campsite on an island in the River Rhone, just across from the famous walls. This sounded pretty interesting and although we were a little dubious about navigating the roads in our camper we decided to go for it. As it turned out, it is a manageable destination and the campsite was perfect. The biggest we had so far stayed at, it was surprisingly quiet and private, its large pitches concealed by magnificent trees. This was at odds with the buzzing walled centre just a 10-minute walk away with its *Palais des Papes* and *Le Pont d'Avignon* and in particular, Nutella crepes made by a cheery street-vendor eaten in a charming square. Isabella was less interested in history and more in this pastime, which meant that although as a couple we could have quite easily used it as a base for a couple of weeks from which to enjoy theatre, art and museums, it was not practical for our situation for more than a day or two. Walking in the easily accessed Provence countryside however, proved to be the perfect family day out.

> It is possible to visit cities with a small baby and a dog; you simply have to be more aware of what you can and can't do. Museums, theatre and restaurants were a no-no, but walking through the cobbled streets enjoying lunch al fresco and Nutella crepes was satisfactory for all the family.

Driving just an hour out of town we parked in the village of Rustrel and set off to walk in the Luberon region, navigating ourselves before we left around the rather basic and unusual village toilet facilities housed in a peculiar stone tower. Be warned that in hindsight I think the back of the truck would have made a better choice for nappy changing. The area is known as Provence's Colorado and until fairly recently was a place where ochre was mined. This has left wonderful orange hues that reveal themselves intermittently beneath the plain rock faces and on a typically sticky early summer's day, the area is a spectacular site when viewed from afar and bordered by beautiful red poppies. The walking book described the difficulty level of this hike as moderate, but after an hour's wrong-turn up a steep hill – sadly I must take complete responsibility for this – it ended up as quite a difficult five-hour trek. For me with a heavy rucksack on my back, Scott with a small but fairly heavy person on his back and Milla a dog who might prefer to lie in the shade, this made it quite an expedition. However, a picnic lunch by the river watching our daughter stumble around gleefully in the long grass chasing butterflies, and an abundance of breathtaking scenery on offer, it was entirely worthwhile. But alas, we knew that our few days with Avignon as our base, although wonderfully varied and enjoyable, were coming to an end. With a young family it was exhausting and finding ourselves out in the open countryside we realised the time was right to let our wheels lead us to a new destination.

Stranded In The South of France

Blue waters sparkling with the richness of diamonds, long, tanned limbs running the length of slender gleaming yachts; the summer playgrounds of famous film stars. Small dogs carried in animal-print handbags, large glasses, high heels, vibrant red lips, even a full netted skirt swinging on curvaceous hips drifted before my eyes. The *Côte d'Azur* is everything you imagine and for a few days it is glorious to indulge in its sights; watch the fancy cars pull up outside the Casino in Monte Carlo, feel the buzz of Monaco marina and walk alongside the yachts. We disappeared into the myriad cobbled alleyways to find a tiny *pâtisserie* tucked away at the end of a narrow row of buildings. Run by two fabulously friendly Italians who cooed over Isabella, plying her with bread sticks and marvelling at her back pack transport, we bought fresh sandwiches before heading off for a picnic on the beach at Antibes – the only place we could find where dogs were accepted.

We had arrived on the south coast several days previously but although we were keen to enjoy the more famous sights, we also wanted to experience the stunning countryside that is so vastly different from the better-known millionaires playground. As a travelling family on a budget we opted to stay further inland and take day trips out to the more flamboyant areas. The campsite we chose was a small, traditional and very French affair not far from the picture postcard town of Roquebrune-sur-Argens. This town stretches from its famous orange rock down to the sea with forest along the way, and includes a quintessentially French centre. Steep cobbled streets wind their way beneath the arches of ancient buildings the colour of sand, farmers' markets show off an array of delicious cheeses, wines and other local produce and powder blue and green shutters stand open to the sunlight, their ledges and wrought iron balconies dripping with bursts of bright flowers. It is about as far from the shimmering *Côte d'Azur* as you can get and for us proved to be a wholesome rural retreat to return to on the days we chose to visit the coast. As we strolled through the streets we enjoyed listening to locals passing the time of day, commenting on each other's vegetables and sharing coffees in the sun and we really felt it was a truly magical place, and also wonderfully friendly, not least because it was here that we found ourselves yet another cheery French mechanic to fix our wagon.

It seemed that the problem we had encountered on the hillside had apparently been slowly caused by something else, so before heading off on our next planned trip to Carcassonne, we were advised to get it fixed. The garage had been recommended to us by the campsite and the mechanic, although extremely forgiving and patient with my French vocabulary and hand actions, could of course do nothing about the week-long wait for the necessary parts. So, cursing ourselves for not putting it in straight away, we quickly followed our rolling eyes with a shrug of the shoulders and thought that there were many worse places in the world to be stranded. We emptied the wagon of our essential items and loaded it all onto our back, put Milla on her lead and proceeded to make the fairly long walk back to our campsite only to stop in our tracks a few seconds later when we heard the mechanic shouting after us, gesticulating with his arms and beckoning us to return, which we duly did. *"Non, non, non,"* he cried *"Vous devez utiliser ce véhicule!"* It makes me smile when I hear people talk about the French not liking the English. There are unfriendly people in every country and I don't think this disposition has much to do with origin. Certainly the French mechanics had been unbelievably nice to us in our plight. In this instance he absolutely refused to watch our family heading off on foot because he worried about how we would cope when we needed to shop for food. Instead he led us round to the back of his garage and produced a battered and bruised silver Fiat and offered it to us to use – for free – until our own wagon was ready! We thanked him profusely and trundled off, a happy Isabella in the back, wind blowing her hair high in the sky and felt thankful and amazed at how the problems you encounter in life often have a way of working themselves out, at best with the help of kind people along the way.

Rainy Days & Playtime

"Never seen rain like this before and we've been holidaying on this campsite for the last 10 years," said one couple we bumped into at the washing up sinks. Comments like this came from French, Dutch, German and English as the sudden downpours, at first thought to be showers, became relentless, stretching out to days and days of sheet rain. Our picturesque pitch of green grass with a river running down below became a mud bath, soggy underfoot. And the river, once low, clear and welcoming to swimsuit-clad bodies in need of refreshment, was instead high and mud coloured. So much rain fell that debris from the famous rock turned the landscape orange and despite being fairly positive people, our spirits began to flag and we wondered, "What are we doing and why?"

Rain is a funny thing. Put me in a sweet chocolate-box cottage in the country with a blazing fire, toasted tea cakes, a good book and a warm coat and boots at the door and I will neither complain nor fail to see beauty in such a landscape. In fact sometimes I simply like to follow my daughter's lead; standing with my face into the rain, my arms spread into the bracing winds. I feel just as I did when I was a child begging my mum to let me out so that I could run up and down the hill to feel the wind and fine rain caress my face. However, when the rain falls outside the window of a camper, four defeated faces pressed to the window, unable to get dry, wash clothes or escape to museums and indoor play parks because of our four-legged friend, it can be a depressing experience. Oh how I wished at that moment I was on the outside looking in. We missed the sunshine, we missed living in a dry warm house, we missed clean clothes and somewhere in between removing collected water from the Dandy roof into a bowl, showering in what was essentially a large shed in the freezing cold and tending to Scott's zillions of mosquito bites we forgot why we had left our old life at all. But, the one thing you cannot afford to be for too long when you are living out a dream, especially with a baby, is miserable and so we had to face the rain head on and keep going.

> The hardest thing for us as a family on the road was when the rain came. The only way to stay cheerful was to dream of what might happen next and think of creative things to do like make giant bouncy castles out of all the cushions or have a music afternoon using every pot, pan, bowl and wooden spoon we could find.

We spent wonderful hours jumping around homemade bouncy castles of cushions and blankets, watching movies on our computer, playing music on pots and pans and baking all together and then, when it looked like the rain might ease a bit, we ventured out to become lost in the mountains. The *Gorge du Verdon* proved the ideal place for a magical walk, with scenery rivalling some of the best I have seen. Spectacular horizons around each corner, huge rock overhangs, free flowing rivers and the village of *La Palud-sur-Verdon,* which was to be the start of our walk. For three hours we crossed these great lands of barren trees, deserted moorland and ruined villages and the only other soul we passed was the postwoman in her little yellow van zipping across the countryside. The walk was magnificent and cleared our minds, which had become foggy and clogged with the damp. It also helped us to conclude that free–spirits are not dampened by the lack of warm baths, insulation more than 1/2′ thick and washing machines. None of these could compare with the open road and the feeling that every day we wanted to stand with our heads out of the sun-roof, arms in the air shouting at the tops of our voices.

The Family Make Hay

Our ability to hang on to every ounce of positivity during the lower points of our travels I am sure has helped us continue our travelling path, although I must hand a large chunk of our next fortune over to fate itself. During the rains I had been reading a book set near Toulouse and the descriptions of the countryside were so vivid, so mesmerising, that I announced to Scott I felt a strong urge to visit that part of France. We checked distances but decided it was quite a detour from our loosely thought-out plan to continue towards Spain via the south coast. At the same time the combination of a strong desire to start meeting inspiring people as well as experience firsthand ways of life that we thought we might want for ourselves had led to my looking for volunteer opportunities on a farm. While the sky hung heavy and grey over our heads we used our time to research on the Internet and I had stumbled upon an advert from a lady looking for helping hands to make hay in SW France. I knew instantly that it was a sign and we were meant to be there and so the day we picked up our car, was the day we made the long drive all the way to a small horse farm in the midi-Pyrenees. We couldn't have waited a minute longer even if we had had to and we chose to not stop halfway for the night, instead hanging firmly on to the image of us relaxing in shadowy green meadows. We were not wrong. Along the south coast we drove before we turned back in to the slow lane. Past walled cities, rolling meadows; farm animals happily munching, until at the end of the day we turned onto a small lane amid the patchwork road system of the rural heart of France and into the yard of a little horse farm 20 miles from the town of Mirande, 100km SW of Toulouse. There was a tractor parked outside the hay barn and huge oak trees sheltered tables and chairs. It was picture perfect. The only unnerving part of our otherwise serene arrival was that the whole family: parents, three daughters and dog, were sitting ready and waiting to check us over and fire questions at our overwhelmed faces. A few glasses of wine later the conversation flowed, a relaxed atmosphere had been established and the start of what would turn out to be two weeks of French farm bliss began.

The first morning I woke early and stepped outside our very luxurious static home accommodation to find myself faced with views of rolling hills to the right, the snow-capped Pyrenees to the left and Milla playing happily in the fields with her new–best friend, Noggin, the farm collie. All the visions Scott and I had shared throughout the early stages of planning our dream resembled moments like this. As I stood there that morning, I knew that this was a place that would capture us with its understated but rich beauty.

> We found this opportunity to volunteer on a farm via a private advert, but we have since discovered Help Exchange (HelpX), an organisation that puts potential volunteers in touch with hosts all over the world. It is based around farming opportunities and if you contact people directly, there is often the opportunity to negotiate terms (usually board and food in return for work) to allow the whole family to take part.

The next two weeks saw us turning fields of grass the old-fashioned way for hay making, Scott was busy logging for hours and in the evenings we cooked family meals together and enjoyed them with good conversation and wine around a big heavy table in the farm kitchen.

Copper pots hung on nails around the walls, fresh flowers sat in stripy pots and the hugest fireplace dominated; even a banjo was at times brought out to provide background music. Isabella was in her element and it was so refreshing to see her running around so happily. Fascinated by the chickens and all the people she was meeting, yet un-phased by it all, the greatest thing was to see her walking so well. She had only just started to put one foot in front of the other as we were leaving the UK, yet since we had been on the road she had not crawled once. We were also invited to several social gatherings that included the local village fete, where food and wine was served on long trestle tables with friends and strangers alike and a brass band jumped up on chairs to play into the dark night sky to the background of fireworks. Then there was a party held in a house that had been converted from an old ruin and sat overlooking the valley. People of many nationalities and from all walks of life arrived and as we sat around watching the sun set and talking to people who were living the life we sometimes dreamed of, Isabella fast asleep in Scott's arms, we were inspired.

Life on the farm was a magical experience and one where we learned lots of new things, not least a true insight into the practicalities of rural life and what dedication it takes to live that way. My love affair with horses was reignited due to the wonderful opportunity of early morning rides where I would soak up the scenery, cross only the paths of goats, ponies and dogs who ventured out of their yards to greet me and lose myself deep within the calming sound of hooves on the soft track beneath. Growing up with a love of horses and having spent most of my spare time as a teenager at the local stables, it had long been a dream of mine to own one. But real life gets in the way and in the absence of such a dream happening for my teenage self, I drifted in a new direction, but always with a longing for the smell of hay, worn tack and the warm nuzzle of a horse's soft muzzle. But, at the farm I realised that having a horse might still be achievable – this thought contented me. In fact we were content because we knew that although our destiny was still unknown, by letting life lead us, things would happen along the way to take us to where we were meant to be. Chance, luck, fate; call it what you want, for us it felt the only way for us to travel, and as we prepared to head over the Pyrenees to Spain, we felt full of hope for the adventures before us.

Alice Griffin

NINE

Viva España!

Fiestas, Siestas & Sangria

We drove silently through the last of SW France in comfortable heat along tiny winding lanes, captivated by the roses creeping up stone cottages, reaching toward the blue sky. We were all calm and lost in thought, a kind of quiet energy bubbling in the car. I knew things were soon to change when we made that small but significant transition to another country – I think we all did, and our mood reflected this anticipation. Everyone knows that things change when you cross that border into Spain, don't they? Like an unexpected 10ft wave capturing me as I float restfully on the water's surface, this mysterious country whips me up within its frenzy the moment I step into it. Grittily elegant, she is flamenco, guitarra, strong feet on a wooden floor; captivating eyes that speak to me every time, making me easy prey in what is always a short seduction.

This time as we entered the North of Spain we were hit with heat, music and dancing, the streets alive with Fiesta. Haro's biggest weekend of the year is during the celebration of *Batalla Del Vino* and although we were unaware of this fact, as soon as we arrived we knew it would be the perfect event to wake us from the peaceful slumber we had drifted into during our stay in the French hay fields. That location fed my quiet side and my mind's desire for solitude and space, Spain at fiesta time captured my hunger for life. When we arrived on Friday night we were lucky to find a pitch on the only campsite in the vicinity, already filled with Spanish partygoers. We pitched up, strapped Isabella into the buggy and headed straight out into the fading light to see what was happening. The streets leading off from the main square where live music and dancing was going on were thronged with old folk, young folk and small folk; the buzz palpable. We stumbled along wine-bar-lined alleyways that rippled with bodies until we happened upon a tiny courtyard where we scrambled for a table, secured Milla's lead to a leg, sat down with a synchronised deep breath and then allowed our bodies to soak it all up. There were children playing around a fountain, families talking animatedly at tables buzzing with the movement of tapas dishes and waitresses juggling trays and meals in time to the guitar music that drifted from open doors. Isabella sat captivated; we all did, and stayed there until the sun began to set slowly behind the decorative spire of a nearby church and old and small folk began to disperse, leaving the youngsters to party on. Darkness came quickly but we strolled back leisurely through the emptying streets strewn with the odd remnants of a party, finding our way back to the camper by moonlight.

I believe wholeheartedly that introducing your child to these kinds of events from a young age can never be a bad thing. We hope Isabella's early awareness of different cultures will stay with her forever.

The party atmosphere bubbled all weekend and we spent most of it somewhere in the middle bewildered but enthusiastic, until on St Pedro's Day, 29 June, the week's festivities reached their climax. Every year hundreds of people dress from top-to-toe in white with red scarves and hike up to a nearby hill where, after a quick religious service, they throw red wine at each other until they are white no more. We watched from the roadside as people stained purple trailed down the hillside on foot and decorated floats. Isabella laughed as tractors beeped at us and the slightly inebriated occupants waved at her vigorously. Apparently it's all to do with land and a dispute with a neighbouring town that dates back to the 10th century, but any trace of the anger and dispute has long since gone, and in its place is a simply wonderful family fiesta. If you're ever in the North of Spain at this time of year then I recommend you drop in to take a look. For us it was a wonderful entry into a new chapter of our travels.

Friends In The Olive Groves

As the partygoers began to drift away, so did we. Our next destination was a small village about one hour north of Seville, not far from Zafra, where a friend had moved a few years previous to live in a 10-acre olive grove. We were desperate to get there and see what it was all about, not least because it was soon to be Scott's birthday and we wanted to spend it with a friend, but at the same time we were determined to get used to that road-trip feeling of having all the time in the world. We set off at a leisurely pace down the west side of Spain towards Extremadura but the days were made uncomfortable by the heat, and travelling was difficult. With nothing much of interest for the family in this vast expanse of Spain, we made a couple of short stops in Salamanca and Tordesillas before deciding we were ready for some rest in the shade of the olive trees.

To watch a country unroll before my eyes over the course of a few days is something I will never get used to. There is something altogether different about viewing the changing landscapes of a new land from a car window - views pass slowly, yet quickly, and on this journey they went from flat and uninspiring, to mountainous and inspiring, to huge empty expanses, until finally we entered the land of wine and olives. And these are the signs of the south: heat which makes it hard to breathe, the purest blue skies that appear to have been painted without variation, and row upon row of vines and olive trees planted in pale sand, their bodies steadfast in regulated rows following the curvatures of hills and mountains.

> One thing we did find is that journeys in the heat were a serious no-no with Isabella and Milla in the car. We had to leave early in the morning or travel through the night to avoid misery and don't forget to carry plenty of water in the car.

We had arranged to meet our friend at a local garage so that she could guide us back to her traditional finca and so we parked and waited until a little moped pulled round into a bay and a helmeted lady in a skirt, one heeled leg attempting to steady the bike, waved frantically at us. It could only be Kari. I had met Kari first at an office temping interview eight years previous and then again through another office job where we worked together for a year. It seemed regular life had been for neither of us because we had both since opted to go off on our own adventures, and it was great to see her again, not least to recharge our batteries and remind ourselves that we were not completely mad to be doing this – there really are plenty of other people living out their own dreams. We duly said a joyous but quick hola through the car window before following her back down a dusty road and over a bridge until we pulled through the gates of her finca. Bliss is the only word I can use. After more than two months in our camper trailing from place to place, to come somewhere that felt like home and let Isabella and Milla run free without restriction was so liberating. They played in the campo for hours during the day, returning to where we sat on the patio only for refreshment of ice-cold water and slices of melon. We all took regular dips in the pool, a rather niftily painted irrigation tank, and it was just wonderful to spend some time relaxing and figuring out our next move.

We talked about what that move might be during the long hot evenings sipping rum and coke on the swing chair. At that point in our travels there was something intoxicating and captivating about being in Spain because we felt a million miles from home. Into my nostrils drifted the smells of hot dust, sun lotion and water seeping into dry ground and my ears captured the sounds, motorbikes, loud Spanish voices echoing through the night sky, crickets, birds and dogs barking in the still air. We knew we would like to lengthen our time here beyond seeing Kari and beyond our next planned trip to the Andalucían mountains to visit another friend, but we weren't sure where or how. But, instead of letting ourselves get bogged down by thinking about the long-term, we decided not to worry and let fate take its course. We did however need to get packed up and be ready to move forward in the short-term and this was a sad event because Isabella had settled in so well and bonded completely with Kari. They had shared stories on the swing chair and every day Isabella would greet Kari's moped as it trundled through the gates from work. Milla too had enjoyed the newfound freedom of the campo. But, we needed to move on, and left Kari's, promising to return for the olive harvest if we were in Spain at the time.

> I say it again and again - there is no need to buy lots of expensive toys! Even at one-year-old Isabella was happy to play in the campo collecting twigs and looking out at the world from the front step of the finca.

To The Mountains

Kari's olive grove melted away in our wing mirrors one morning as the sun was just starting to peep through the dark sky. Our last night had been spent preparing a meal and chatting in the kitchen. We had watched the orange sunset disappear behind the distant hills and recognised that this place would always be a home from home, somewhere to rest when we needed to. But now we were moving on to search for new delights in the Andalucían Mountains.

Nine years before this I had spent time living in Japan and had become firm friends with a lady who taught at the International School. We met at a party, got talking and eventually organised a weekly girlie night, which had me cycling up the village to her home for a tearjerker movie washed down with a bottle of white. We enjoyed mah-jong and plum brandy evenings with friends and talked for many hours; a firm friendship formed. Penny was an inspiration to me then, and remains so, due to her interesting and varied life and her journey as a woman certainly not afraid of travelling the world alone. We had always kept in touch by email and she stayed with me several times on visits to the UK, but I had not seen her for five years. During that time she had moved from Japan to Egypt and bought a small house in a tiny village in Spain, and I had settled down with a family. As Scott and I had known that Spain was on our itinerary, we had arranged it so that we would be able to meet Penny there to catch up on these major events. We had no real idea of what to expect, knew only the name of the village and had in our possession one blurred photograph showing the outside of the house.

We took off in search of this place and were happy that we did because the seven-hour drive from Zafra to Almeria Province offered us some of the most breathtaking scenery we had seen in Spain so far. We drove higher and deeper into the mountains, huge hunks of rock dominating us, our shape small beneath the shadows. We marvelled at the beautiful towns and villages in the distance and craned our necks to see the cave houses on the outskirts of Granada until we ended up on a tiny winding road towards a small village. As we turned off the main road and onto a dusty track that guided us further and further into the hills, we wondered what we might find. In the rugged rural landscape it was hard to imagine that life went on but then we turned one final corner and the daintiest village stretched up its church spire and drew us in toward its white-washed walls and surrounding fertile land worked by the hands of its residents. We knew instantly that we had arrived somewhere that would become very special to us.

There is only one main road in and out of Almendra and it widens in the middle of the village directly outside the bar where locals congregate every day. We arrived on a Saturday and many tanned and hardy farmers faces sat around plastic tables outside eyeing us suspiciously, although they were happy to wave. We stopped the wagon and sat nervously for a while trying to work out how we might attempt to ask if anyone could help us find Penny's house. But before we could step out of the car a man leapt forward, his darkened complexion that of someone who had worked outside in this heat for many years and the strangest thing happened. Completely unexpectedly a London accent came out of his mouth and he gesticulated towards the left: "If you're looking for Penny then you need to take the next left." It obviously was not difficult to spot lost tourists looking for an English friend and thus, on his direction, we turned our truck left to venture along the tiniest of alleyways in search of her. I jumped out and ran up the street until I saw what looked to be the terracotta building of the photo and called up to the outside terrace to which Penny greeted me. We embraced and she met Scott, Isabella and Milla for the first time and welcomed us into her home, which was the most wonderful place: a cute and traditional village house with outside terrace, open fire, cellar and various little nooks and crannies just waiting to be explored. We sat out late into the evening over dinner and wine, catching up on the intervening years before retiring for a peaceful night's sleep.

On our first morning in Almendra we woke up to the light streaming through the wooden shutters and I immediately jumped out of bed to soak up the view of the sun rising across the hills. I was very excited at the prospect of spending some time here to rest, gather our thoughts and discover. Isabella headed off to the bakery hand-in-hand with Penny first thing and we ate a breakfast of goat's cheese, olives and fresh bread before we went on a guided tour of the village and discovered that it had all anyone would need: a bar that served cheap beer and good food, a bakery where you could buy fresh bread every morning and a soon-to-be-opened general store. We knew pretty much instantly that we would love to spend some time in this peaceful, unspoilt place and each evening we pondered this as we sat reading on the terrace wall with a nightcap, looking up at times to admire the mountain views directly on each side of us and enjoying the silence. There had been a point several months previous when we were preparing to leave life in the UK that we had said to each other, "I wonder when the moment will come that we turn to each other and say 'I'm glad we did this'?" That moment had definitely arrived.

Making Friends

Penny, sensing the almost instantaneous hold Almendra had on us, was quick to suggest that maybe we should look to spend the winter in Spain looking after her Spanish abode? She was due to head back to her home in Egypt at the end of the month and figured that it was always best to have someone in a home rather than leaving it standing empty. When she first mentioned this, although it was appealing, we had been convinced that our travels were likely to take us back to France to rent for the winter. However, we simply hadn't bargained to be so attracted to Spain that we would want to stay and strangely we actually felt like agreeing to take such an opportunity. And so the idea bubbled in the back of our minds over the coming week as we tried to absorb as much of Almendra as possible so we would make the right decision when the time came. The idea of a quiet, uninterrupted winter appealed, but we also realised that it might start to feel quite lonely and we wondered if really, in the true light of day, that might become a problem. What seems like an idyllic place may offer nothing for a one-year-old and so we had some careful thinking to do. Sensing our indecisiveness Penny quickly set up a blind date at the local bar with the only other English family in the village.

> If you plan to spend a few months abroad you will need to consider carefully what this might mean for your young child/children. If you don't know anyone you might feel daunted but I can assure you there is always a park or a nursery in a nearby town where you can go, armed with a dictionary. If your child is very small you might think about hooking up with fellow expat mums in the area. Although the idea of only mixing with locals is romantic and authentic, as a young mother in a strange land I have found it is important to have a few friends who share your language.

At 1pm on Sunday we pulled open the heavy wooden doors, left the peace, quiet and sunshine behind us and entered inside the dark village bar dominated by a huge open fire, raucous laughter and customers enjoying family dinners. This is a marked difference between us Brits and Spaniards. We get our white bits out the moment the weather looks even a little bit like summer, whereas Spaniards go inside to keep cool. Only crazy people would sit outside during the day they think, and so we had the very peculiar experience to be inside in the dark when outside it was bright and blue. The barman quickly beckoned us in with a welcoming smile and we ordered *tinto veranos* in our best Spanish.

Soon the English family joined us and it turned out that dad, Jason, was actually the guy with the London accent who had first spotted us and guided us to Penny. He was as full of life now as he had been then and as his wife, Cresta, moved to his side we noticed four gorgeous boys, including a set of triplets, clinging to their legs. I shot a look to Scott which said, "Playmates for Isabella through the cold and quiet winter months." And instant friends for us too as we immediately hit it off with Jason and Cresta, chatting away as the kids sat around a table being plied with cheese and crisps by the barman's wife. It was obvious immediately that Jason, Cresta and their family had been embraced by the village because everyone knew who they were and their ability to partake in lively Spanish banter revealed their 10 years of living in Spain. They seemed like the perfect family for us to have nearby and any of the doubts we had had about spending the winter in Almendra were blown out of the window. It felt as though this was where our travels were meant to stand still, for a while anyway.

> Spanish bars are different. They are family orientated, but people can and do smoke happily around children. You need to be aware of these factors before you head inside a Spanish bar and if it upsets you, don't go.

Alice Griffin

TEN

Captured by Almendra

We Just Couldn't Leave

It was the air, the silence, the escape from everything we had considered normal and although we were unsure whether Spain would have anything to offer us long-term, at that point it had everything we desired. The views varied with each change of weather, each hand movement of the clock, and I realised very quickly that when you have the time to ponder, to watch, to notice then you do. On a sunny day the mountains were so still they looked superimposed against the blue sky, and when the sun rose and set they would become home to myriad colours, spectacular shadows casting themselves across the surrounding land. If the weather chose to misbehave they would only be visible at certain points through thick puffs of dark and misty cloud and being 1,000 metres above sea level and swamped by their majestic presence was quite something for us ex-city dwellers.

Some mornings I would be up at the crack of dawn working, and I would enjoy the moment as mine. Then, as the sun started to stretch its face above the mountains the village would begin to stir beneath soft golden light. Before long I would hear the villagers waking up, scurrying off towards their vegetable patches; guys in converted rotavators would chug along at a snail's pace, holding cigarettes in their grimy fingers. Women in old shirt-dresses and aprons pushed their empty wheelbarrows ready to fill up with produce and I lapped up the simplicity of this life. So vastly different to the heavy din of motorway traffic that had once filled my ears day and night, the constant stream of trucks and cars that beeped and screeched their way overhead as I walked my dog in the quiet early morning spaces I had found for myself in a busy world. In Almendra I didn't need to search for these spaces - they were available in abundance, and I liked it.

Eventually our own house would awaken and we would embark in a leisurely way on the day's activities. In our previous world we would be rushing around with no time to really think about each task, but in Almendra the pace was slow and it helped us to realign with the very essence of life. Our days were taken up mostly with walking, foraging for food such as figs to make jam, and meeting Cresta and the boys at the park where us mothers would enjoy a cold beer, put the world to rights and watch the children play. I would try to imagine hanging out at the park in England, cold beer in hand and thought that this would probably be seen as irresponsible, but in Almendra it was so quiet, so safe and so away from everything that it was perfectly fine. And then, not long after settling in, Jose the neighbour came round to invite us to the village Fiesta so we could officially meet the whole village. Up to that point we had met a few people, such as the lady next door who would bring us fresh eggs each morning or the old couple down the way who offered us fresh vegetables on a Sunday and biscuits to Isabella each time we walked past their house. We had found everyone to be so friendly, as well as extremely forgiving about our limited Spanish. But now it was time to put ourselves out there because no doubt everyone was hoping to get a peek at the new foreigners in town and find out what our story was.

> Be aware that Spanish time means that any sense of routine will go out of the window, but you might be surprised at how adaptable babies are and also at their ability to sleep amidst unbelievable noise. Buggies are also a great steadying contraption at local Fiestas!

We arranged to meet Jason and Cresta outside the bar; we were glad they had asked us to meet them as it made our arrival a bit more comfortable. The arranged time was 10.30pm, which we found hilarious. In our normal life we would be safely tucked up in bed with a good book, but with the heat of the day gone it is late at night when the party really starts in Spain and children are just as welcome, if not more, than adults. A little tired, we pushed Isabella down to meet our friends and her friends, who were all neatly perched in their double buggies. We drank some beers and watched the place fill up, ready for the village festivities. Everyone was in their finery and by the time we left the bar at midnight to walk down to the square for the actual Fiesta, the place was buzzing. All the locals were out in force dancing the *paso doble* and having a wonderful time and so we all joined in, badly, getting into the spirit of things. The night expanded, and we were bought drinks by new friends and the bar landlord while

Isabella and her friends slept soundly despite the music, waking occasionally to squint at the spectacle unfolding. By 3.30 in the morning we weren't dancing around handbags, we were dancing around buggies and much fun was had until I had to admit defeat and leave the 70-year-old locals to it. We felt buoyant, accepted and on a high from the buzz of actually living in such a place and that night was one of the many when I looked around and thought, "This place, this time, will always have somewhere special in my heart."

Winter In The Mountains

Summer turned to autumn and now we had time to watch the seasons change. The heat dispersed and the sky above the mountains was a cooler shade of blue, less piercing than it had been in the summer. Landscapes at every bend were greener and vegetable patches flourished all around the village. And the air, oh how I miss that Autumn air of Almendra, for it felt crisp on my face yet remained warm on my body. On our morning walks we would pass people daily, all busy harvesting their patches. Peppers, aubergines, chard, courgettes, pomegranates, almonds; food was in abundance and we were lucky enough to receive much. Not a few days would pass without a knock at the door and one person or another would be stood there, arms heavy with something fresh for us, or sometimes it would be Juana from next door holding up the front of her apron cradling eggs. We watched as people went about preserving their bounty; dried figs from a neighbour, charcoaled peppers hot from the fire at the back of the bakery. We ate them like that, but soon they would be bottled by the local women who sat in circles peeling away the charred skins and chatting for hours. I realised that this is how people survive in small communities. They may not have much material wealth, but they have food and crafting skills and share these, ensuring that nobody goes without the necessities of life.

> There was no doubt that Isabella was a real ticket to our acceptance into daily village life. The Spanish adore children and new life arriving in the village was something that they embraced.

Isabella was loved by all and our fears of there not being enough for her to do were unfounded. When she wasn't out playing in the yard she was being plied with treats by villagers or playing at the park with her friends and there were many other things going on in our new life. Every Sunday was family afternoon at the bar with Jason and Cresta, or sometimes egg sandwiches on their terrace staring at the view and chatting. Two mornings a week we would wander down the dry riverbed (which doubled up as a road until the water started to flow in late winter) to visit a local dog rescue centre. We would spend two hours there, walking some of the 50+ dogs and hanging out with the horses. Isabella loved being around all the animals, as did Milla. We picked blackberries and figs to make jams and cheesecakes with so that we had something to give back to those who fed us, and we welcomed visitors into our new life. These were my parents, my oldest friend and her daughter, followed by Scott's dad who arrived just as Autumn started to turn to winter and the whole place rested uncharacteristically under a thick blanket of snow. It was a fun time and we enjoyed sharing our life with family and even though some might have thought our path a little strange, they could see how much we were thriving, instantly sensing the warmth of our new community.

Despite the occasional rains and the one blast of thick snow, the sky remained blue and the temperature comfortable, so we would often go for picnics at Lake Negratin, a magnificent reservoir surrounded by a spectacular lunar-like landscape. It reminded me of my visit to the Grand Canyon. Back then I had risen at 4am to drive to this spectacular place and watch the sun come up across the rocks and marvel at the changing colours. It had been a very peaceful experience, awe-inspiring, and although Lake Negratin was very small in comparison, dependent on the time of day and the weather, the rocks gave glints of many hues just as they did in Arizona. There was also a mountain range that we loved to go where we could walk, picnic and feel a sense of peace and we went there regularly right through to December. Looming high and dominating the skyline from the village we would snake upwards between jagged rocks, looking down into deep pine-filled gorges before continuing higher towards an old mining town that was left deserted many years before. Now you can wander through the ruined buildings that crumble gently amidst the breathtaking landscape and this is where we would set our blanket down, lie back and just lose ourselves in the silence.

> I know that it is common sense, but on one visit to Lake Negratin we actually forgot to take a spare set of clothes for Isabella. We still let her take a dip (how could we not?) and instead fashioned a sari from my jumper to keep her warm afterwards. One thing I have found on our travels is that being creative is key to solving many little hiccups along the way!

We had settled into a steady pace of life over the autumn and winter months and we enjoyed the simplicity. Spain in the winter, when you are inland away from the tourist destinations, is a place vastly different to the clichés. It is rich with natural beauty, many people alive with compassion and for us it felt like home for that time in our life.

Olive Picking In Extremadura

Standing in an olive grove, silently and steadily my hands work shiny black fruits from their branches. The sky is a still, crisp blue and the leaves of the trees appear motionless against it. There's a quiet whistling in the distance, an amalgamation of pueblo noise: dogs, children, clatter, chatter and beneath me the soft thud of olives tumbling into my basket. I think to myself, "have I ever felt such calmness in my soul?" and consider that the answer is probably no. There is something so back to basics, so organic, so authentic about working land. It removes all pretences of life, strips us bare of the world we build around ourselves and takes us back to the only thing that really matters – nature.

Our latest journey had started on an early Saturday morning when we left our little village at 6am for a journey across Spain to go back to Kari's olive farm in Extremadura. We had agreed to help her with the harvest and as we had all so loved our time there we couldn't wait to go back for a week's working holiday. Driving in darkness we watched the sun break the night sky, passed through the snow-capped Sierra Nevada and negotiated the bustle of lunchtime Seville, before we emerged on the other side into rolling valleys carpeted in green, simple white fincas interrupting the skyline. When we arrived, Kari's son, Aaron, was there with his friend, Dean and much fun was had as we worked our way around the 400 olive trees, moving our baskets and nets to catch the fruit as we went. The boys worked together and as they moved further and further in one direction, Kari and I listened to their noisy banter and laughter drift away as we moved in the other, choosing to pick silently. Isabella of course headed straight for the boys' end of the field and was made very welcome. She would lie under the tree sorting the leaves from the fruit as well as picking the low olives and putting them into her own bag. As we were potty training Isabella at that time, being up in the top field meant we were quite a way from the house and the loo, so we simply took her potty with us and placed it under an olive tree. This caused much laughter, but we remained accident-free that week.

> On the road and in many new locations we still had various obstacles to get over e.g. potty training, but with a little imagination and forethought, you can manage perfectly successfully.

And so our week was spent picking, all the time indulging in spectacular views of the pueblo whose whitewashed buildings protruded from the olive grove before melting backward into the rising hills. Jose, Kari's neighbour, would lumber toward the fence to discuss in deep cheerful Spanish tones how the picking was going. Children from a neighbouring family bombed up and down the lane on bikes shouting, "*Hola!*" before eventually plucking up the courage to come and help, once they spotted Kari in the field with us. Their mother's calls rang across the campo, checking to make sure they were safe. And as we stood there, picking and bumbling along in broken Spanish, I thought to myself how many special moments our travels had given us as a family and how different these early years of Isabella's life might have been had we stayed in our life in England.

Of course, all workers must rest and once free of our mud-caked wellies, our scratched arms bathed, we would enjoy our evenings together, taking turns to cook family meals at the finca; talking, laughing, playing dominoes and watching Aaron do magic tricks, or heading into the local village for cold beers. The bar was always full – with children and parents alike. Faces beamed and people talked animatedly through swirling plumes of cigarette smoke and the tab was run on either an excellent memory, or simple old-fashioned honesty. At the weekend we headed to Zafra, aptly referred to as Little Seville, which lies at the foot of the Sierra de Castellar. Here there were eateries and bars with all the hustle and bustle required for a Saturday night, although it was still very much a family-orientated place. I've never before been to a city bar late on a Saturday night where staff and customers have no problem with a toddler gleefully chucking paper napkins around for entertainment!

> Throughout Spain we found that all bars and restaurants were child-friendly and nobody batted an eyelid at Isabella's presence; it is the norm for families to venture out all together of an evening.

We were sad when the time came to return to Almendra because a real family unit had developed within the walls of Kari's home and we had all settled into our task.

Most of all we had had such fun, not least Isabella who had fallen in love with Dean and clung to him for the entire olive harvest. It was with some reluctance, but safe in the knowledge that we would be back again, that we packed up the wagon, said our goodbyes and returned to what had now become our normal life.

Plans To Move On

In the months we spent in Almendra we left several times for trips away, but we always enjoyed returning to what had become a retreat for us, a place where we could escape from the life that had once been ours and think clearly. In many ways we relished the idea of living simply and quietly and embraced the days of making jam, growing herbs, doing yoga on the terrace, much to the enjoyment of our neighbours, and reading more books than we had been able to in a long time. We had also become accustomed to our lengthy daily walks with Milla and Isabella, soaking up the mountain views and breathing in the fresh air; in fact we had all settled comfortably into a steady routine. Even our appearance had become more familiar to the locals and they would now stop and talk to us and explain things at length so we were picking up the language. There was the old boy who we would watch every single morning as he scythed crops to feed his horses. We would often walk back up the dusty track with him mumbling in broken Spanish, a challenge due to the fact that he was hard of hearing! And then there was the man who must have been over 90, who would often pull up alongside us in his electric car, extend his weathered hand out of the window and let a gleeful Isabella choose one of the brightly-wrapped sweets in his palm, their wrappers glinting in the sunlight.

We had learned to love the fact that popping to the local shop would always become an hour-long mission due to all the conversations that would take place along the way and we marvelled at our neighbour who cared for his donkey at the back of his tiny house, a man who in his day had walked many miles to work in the mines hidden high in the mountains. There were also people who our hearts felt a true fondness for - such as Juana, who had kept us in eggs for most of our stay; her friendly face and compassionate disposition welcomed us warmly every time we stepped out of our door each morning. Then in Isabella's heart a space had been cleared for the elderly couple down the road who doted on her, and whose door we could not pass without being invited in for treats of some description. So many faces, so many smiling eyes had welcomed us, strangers, into their community.

But, throughout all this many evening conversations were woven, about our future, about what was best for us as a family and we always knew that as much as Almendra had found its way into our hearts, we could never settle there. This had been an opportunity to enter a community, to feast our eyes on the breathtaking scenery and live a life very different from what we had known, fulfilling our dreams of travel and experience. There was still much more we wanted to do; although we had achieved our goal of exploring and spending more family time together, ideas of heading off around Italy, Greece and Eastern Europe were shelved because we still longed to consider more long-term options. We had pangs for a home to call our own again. Granted, we were very sure that we wanted a different life for our family, but we were still seeking some continuity, some level of stability, and thought back to the beginning of our dreams and why we had chosen to pack up and leave our life in England.

> When you travel with a young child in countries such as Spain you will instantly become aware of the locals' love for children. You should be prepared to accept many gifts in every shop you enter, from bread rolls to lollypops and even a bag of raisins from cashiers in supermarkets. And it will always add time on to any planned shopping trip!

Our original thought way back, before we embarked on this road trip, had been that maybe we could start a new life in France on a little land where we could keep some animals, but we had not tried this yet, so we decided to look for a long-term opportunity via the volunteer network, HelpX. After many emails bouncing to and from various hosts we eventually secured a placement at a vegetarian hotel and restaurant in Normandy. Scott would be caring for the animals, working the land and preparing the hotel for the season, and in return we would have a house to live in for a few months. It seemed like the perfect next step and after much deliberation about whether the time was right to get back in the wagon and wind our way back through Spain to the rolling green meadows of France, we finally decided that it was. Almendra had become familiar, it was a comfort to us, but we didn't wish to get to the point of failing to see its beauty because we had stayed too long. No, I wanted to remember the time we had spent there with joyous clarity; hold the memories in my heart. And so, with some reluctance, we began telling our friends and neighbours that soon we would be leaving to continue on our journey.

Sad Farewells

I will never forget the morning we left Almendra. The village was bathed in early light, each building, every person surrounded by a feathery glow. We rose early and loaded the last of our belongings into the wagon with heaviness in our hearts, but at the same time joyfully anticipating the next leg of our journey. Outside were neighbours and locals, all keen to see us off, but the hardest person to say goodbye to was Juana who cried when she hugged us tightly and wished us all well. In the village new life is celebrated and young families mean a continued community, so our departure was sad to some who maybe had thought we would settle there. As we drove away past the bar that had welcomed us so warmly on many Sunday afternoons we beeped the horn and as we approached the end of the village I made Scott stop the car. I jumped out and took one last picture of the mountains in the distance, the orange sun poking above, throwing thick bands of light across the whitewashed buildings of the village. As we turned the corner into the very last part of the village I felt sick, but there was still one more stop to make.

I knocked on Cresta's door, which she opened slowly, her hand shielding the light from her eyes, the boys all running around still in their pyjamas. We hugged and I could contain the tears no more. They lasted until we had left Almendra way, way behind us. I hadn't expected to feel quite so emotional about the whole thing but so much had happened for us there. One of Isabella's first words had been *hola*, some of her first memories had been made in Almendra and we were leaving behind good friends with whom we had shared many drinks, meals and laughs. Life there had treated us well, but we knew that it would not be the first, nor the last, difficult goodbye we would make on our travels and so we trundled off watching yet another home fade away in the wing mirror, its image blurred by my water-filled eyes.

I want to feel life, reach out and touch it, collect as many memories as I can along the way so that whenever I close my eyes my mind is always a colourful montage of landscapes, faces and feelings. I want to look back and know that every single day I stayed true to myself, and my family, doing whatever I felt was the best thing. With this desire comes change and with change comes tears; but underneath those tears a nervous excitement simmers and my hope on the morning we left Almendra was that with another leap into the unknown, we would be entering a future filled with many more adventures.

Where To Next?

The continuing story... Every tale must reach its close and choosing the end for my story was difficult, but as I wrote about our departure from Almendra I realised from that point our travels changed entirely. I wanted to keep writing, to share with you the adventures that unfolded, but it had become a whole new story. We were no longer simply travelling for travel's sake; we were looking for a place to put down roots, as a base for short-term travels. Thus, this book covers the first two years only of travels with my family.

Maybe one day I will write a book about trying to find the right place to settle with your child! I would tell you about our months spent in France, caring for poultry and sheep, where Isabella started her own journey at a local nursery, as well as the road trip which saw us purchase Elvis, a more luxurious home on wheels, and head off to the NW of Spain and on to Portugal. In this fascinating country Isabella helped build a yurt, rode her first horse, ran freely through vineyards and swam alongside us in rivers. However, our quest for a place to call home eventually brought us back to England, but far from where we had lived before: to the North Yorkshire countryside, which is where we are now. We go out foraging for food, enjoy many walks through the windswept moors and in particular we love to eat ice-creams on the sandy beaches of this rugged coastline. Sometimes I think our travels with Isabella have helped us to appreciate the wonder in our own country, although ask me if this is where we will stay and I'm afraid I still don't know. What I do know is that we have no fear of heading off with our beautiful daughter in tow and wherever we decide to settle, we know we will always keep travelling. Now nearly three Isabella remains a delight to have with us and embraces our nomadic lifestyle. Our future travel plans include an Eastern-Europe and Scandinavia road trip, followed by Canada and Alaska, then hopefully Southeast Asia; I feel nothing but excitement about showing these parts of the world to her as she grows. It is hard to imagine my old life travelling solo; it would be such a shame not to have Isabella by my side, eyes glinting, cheeks rosy, a small arm sliding behind my neck whispering, "Look, Mummy! Pretty! Me lucky!" This world is a gift, I believe that, and to be in awe of its beauty and feel lucky to experience it, for me, is the most precious lesson I can teach my daughter.

I suppose my own desire and appreciation of travel undoubtedly came from my parents who over the years have been known to embark on many unorthodox trips by road, plane and boat during their early years of parenting, as well as beyond. I only hope that their ability to do such trips with more than one child will be a skill passed on to me. There are no plans for more babies, but if they do come along I very much doubt that I will stop our independent travelling even then. No, I hope that just like my parents, life will continue to lead me into the arms of an exciting and awe-inspiring world. As I write these final words I am preparing to wave them off on a nine-week journey to America and New Zealand, where they will be navigating the roads themselves in a camper. Not bad for a couple of 70 year olds.

Happy Travels!
Alice

Inspirational Stories
...from Other Travelling Mums

Introduction by Alice

I would now like to pass this final chapter over to four mums who I have been fortunate enough to meet while working on this project. Tanya travels long-term with her children, homeschooling along the way, Tina talks about her experience as a single mum on a budget vacationing in London, Gail is a trailing spouse who has lived and travelled worldwide with her children and Linda travels broadly within her home country of England. I hope this demonstrates the many different ways you can make travel a small, or big, part of your family life, tailoring it to suit your own lifestyle, budget and desires.

Tanya Whitehead

Tanya Whitehead graduated with an Honours degree in Journalism from Rhodes University, South Africa in 1992 and is a freelance writer. You can catch up with her travels and blog on **www.savayla.wordpress.com** She home schools her two daughters Savannah and Ayla using Enki Education whilst travelling around South East Asia. She is currently living in Langkawi, Malaysia, but this could change at any moment, as she and her husband Kyle Watkins have their eyes on spending a few months in New Zealand before heading to Australia. Kyle is a software developer who doesn't like the same view every day, so works while he travels. He is lucky that his clients don't mind whether he sits under a coconut tree or in a formal office, as long as his work is delivered on time.

I remember the first time we decided to chuck it all and go and find our utopia. Savannah was two and a half, and Ayla 12 months old. Two toddlers, two backs, four hands and a McLaren double pram. New Zealand was our final destination, but we were first going to backpack around South East Asia for a while. Everyone thought we were completely insane and opinions were given.

We, however, knew ourselves and our girls, and thought it would be a fantastic adventure. We travelled for 10 months, three of these in New Zealand, the rest around Singapore, Thailand and Malaysia by plane, train, bus, taxi, ferry, and long tail boat. There were no regrets. Kids are so easy to travel with, especially if they are being breastfed, as Ayla was. They are also your passport to different people and experiences in these foreign and exotic countries.

The best item that I could have taken with me was the McLaren double pram. One of those that have both seats next to each other and fits through a single door. When one child was tired, we lay the seat flat so she could sleep, while the other was still jabbering away. It was fairly light and quick to put up and down, which paid off when we were woken up at 5am on our train trips across South East Asia (SEA), to have our passports stamped, and had to put sleeping babes into it, then get back onto the train. The next best things were their small dolls and a packet of Duplo. I have always travelled with my Red Cross Hospital Book for children as it is like having a doctor with us at all times.

Go forward five years to November 2008 and we were leaving South Africa again, after spending three years living on a small wooden yacht. We had decided to give up our friends and family and leave South Africa because of the rising crime and fear that we experienced all the time. Destination, South East Asia. This time, we were calling it our Year of Discovery. We did not know where we would end up, New Zealand was still in our hearts, but our three years on the yacht in Cape Town had put us off rain and cold weather. We were going to try Thailand first and then see what happened. Savannah was almost eight by now, and Ayla was six and a half. It was a completely different ball game as I was now home schooling and this would have to continue, and fit into our bags. Out went the nappies and pram; in went sturdy walking shoes and books. We bought each of the girls their own small suitcase on wheels, one they could handle themselves, with lots of zipped pockets for all their little items. I packed their homeschool books and their clothes and the rest of the space was for their toys.

They had to think carefully and took most of their small animals, Polly Pockets, a Barbie and one fluffy toy. Trust me, they do not need to take all their favourite toys, as you collect along the way.

We spent a wonderful two months in Thailand, starting South in Phuket for five weeks and then heading North to Chiang Mai. We tend to spend longer stretches in one place as we discover an area and get the feel for it. Our general criteria are price, internet and swimming pool or garden for the girls. We found all of that and more in Shanti's Lodge in Ao Nang, Phuket, and Cave Lodge in Soppong, Northern Thailand. A kid's paradise. A two-week trip that took us along the Chiang Mai, Pai, Mae Hong Son Loop was to be our favourite voyage, and the one which the girls remember the best. Elephant jungle trekking, riding down rivers in bamboo rafts, driving up to the Burmese border, spending Xmas in a remote village where Father Christmas wrapped his small presents in banana leaves, and watching the villagers roast the chicken and vegetables, bake the Xmas cake and dinner rolls in an outside wood-fired earth oven. All the local kids were there and even though there was a language barrier, this did not stop the girls from playing in the hammocks and swimming with these village kids in the icy cold river below. We were also invited to a local Lisu tribe wedding, which involved hours of all the guests tying money around the bridal couple's wrists. The girls always wore their special local clothes for these occasions. They learnt to sleep in odd sized beds and mattresses on the floor, never complaining, as it was part of the adventure. Once they slept in a tent which had proper mattresses and duvets, on the banks of a river outside Mae Hong Son, listening to the elephants squeal and roar further down.

During all this travel I did not school much nor stress about it. Savannah was always reading and figuring out the maps and Ayla spent her time drawing. They were immersing themselves into each place and that was good enough for me. We spent three months living in Kota Kinabalu, Sabah, Borneo and from there we made the decision that although we loved SEA, we needed more for the girls and ourselves, so decided to emigrate to Australia. This is a lengthy process so we opted to travel some more and headed for Langkawi, Malaysia, hoping that this would be our final stop until Australia.

We have been in Langkawi for six months now. As I write this we have started a new global cultures home schooling curriculum, Enki, which the girls and I are thoroughly enjoying, and I try and find excursions that fit in with the subject of our home schooling. So, on a recent trip to Singapore, I took them to visit the Ethiopian village at the zoo so they could experience an African hut and implements as they are doing an African block for school and we spent some time at the snow zone as this year we are focusing on extreme weather conditions. I also introduced them to the Krishna temple and Little India as we are going to be doing a block on Ghandi and Mirabai later on in the year. As it is coming up to Deepavali soon (festival of light) the temple and Little India town was in a flurry of ceremonies, music, incense and colourful decorations. The girls have also experienced the full monsoon season here, including seeing places flooded and learning why the locals should still be building their houses on stilts. It is a small island, only 50,000 people, water buffalo, rice paddy fields, coconut palms and jungle covered mountains. We have allowed our children to foster some kittens and they were allowed to witness them being spayed and neutered. They know how to eat with chopsticks, use a squat toilet without peeing on their feet or getting their pants wet, sing with the water buffalo calves, wake up at 4am for breakfast during Ramadan fasting days, appreciate amazing sunsets, play in the rain, sleep anywhere, wake up early, go to sleep late, eat late, count in three different languages, wear local clothes, play with kids of all nationalities, go to the *pasar malam* (night market) and choose their own food and pay for it. They have been to a Muslim, Kadazan and Lisu wedding.

Although they are too young to understand the whole world dynamic, they are living it. By getting to know people from various countries and ethnic backgrounds, they have learnt not to judge people by their skin colour or religion, but by their attitudes and actions. I think this is the most important factor for me, especially coming from such a racially divided country as South Africa. So far they have made friends with Australians, Indians, Chinese, Korean, Pakistan, American, Malay, British and Swiss and are really living and experiencing the full rainbow, and yet they don't make these distinctions like I do. They just accept everything as it is - one benefit of homeschooling I could not teach them. Only travelling and living in different countries has done that.

Things we took that were invaluable:

- McLaren Pram
- Essential oil spray for bed bugs and toilet seats
- Readers Digest Red Cross Children's Ailments book

- Wet wipes
- Lavender essential oil
- Tea Tree essential oil
- Natural products for burns, bites, diarrhoea, teething, bladder infections (NB for girls)
- A sense of humour

Tina Norman

Tina Norman is mum to one son. When he was small she decided that even though she was a single mother, travel could still play an important part in family life and thus she adapted trips to suit their needs, location and budget. Here she talks about a short vacation in the city of London. Tina continues to write about her life at: **www.haveitalltoday.blogspot.com**

When my son was four years old, his dad and I separated. I moved out and my son began his routine of shuttling from one parent to the other, so that he'd spend equal time with us. I've always known that this isn't the storybook start to a childhood, and I was determined that I would do everything in my power to give him the best time I could. He was little, but he'd try really hard to understand what was going on, why his mum and dad lived in different houses and why toys were always at the wrong house. It seemed to me that one of the ways to maintain an air of normality was to travel with him. As a single mother, my budget didn't stretch very far, but the sheer joy of seeing places through my son's eyes has been worth every penny.

The first year I was on my own I decided it was really important to take D on holiday, but that left me with a bit of a dilemma. I don't drive, I didn't have very much money, and I needed to find somewhere that would be able to keep a four-year-old occupied. I'm sure there were lots of places to choose from, but my brain was a bit fuddled at best, and I decided to take him to London for five days. We had the most fabulous time ever.

I chose London because there's a direct rail link to Euston from where I live, and then I chose a hotel I could safely haul a small child and a large suitcase to. Oh, and which was in my price range, had a roof, and with a room I didn't need to share with three other families. I'd very rarely been to London before, and was petrified of getting lost, losing my son or being mugged/stabbed/sold into slavery so I decided that we'd eat in the hotel to reduce any or all of those eventualities. Having survived the first night remarkably well (a family room is surprisingly spacious when there's only two of you, and most hotels seem a bit sniffy about offering single parents anything smaller), we decided to hit the tourist trail.

I had nothing but admiration for London after that. We got our little book of tube tickets.

If you try to get through the turnstile without buying a ticket for your child, pick them up and carry them. (Don't squeeze them through first then try to get through yourself – your child will spend the remainder of the journey convulsed with laughter at mummy's bottom being jammed). We visited the Natural History Museum, the London Eye, went on a river boat cruise, we saw Buckingham Palace. We had a great time at London Zoo, went to see the Lion King, wandered round Covent Garden and St James Park. We packed so much into those five days that all my plans for catching up on my reading when D went to bed disappeared into the ether and I tumbled into bed about half an hour after he did every night.

Of course, it cost more money than I'd anticipated. Any mother knows that even when you take your child to a free attraction, the payoff arrives in the gift shop when your child has to have a pencil, a key ring, a postcard or a packet of sweets in the shape of the Tower of London. But the museums are free, the walks in the park cost nothing, and the sheer fun of spending time together is absolutely priceless.

Gail Mowat

Gail Mowat gave up her fledgling career as a newspaper brand manager in the UK aged 26 and has since worked as a translator and editor, internet television news presenter, estate agent, caterer, copy writer, freelance travel hack and tried her hand as a small-scale retailer. In between these efforts she had three children who are now eight, six and one. She currently lives in Kazakhstan, is a freelance writer and runs a hobby blog about her life in the former-CIS at **www.bigbelugababy.blogspot.com**. She is currently setting up a travel blog with a travel-editor, and mum-of-three friend called **www.familytravelexpert.com**. Gail will handle Rest of the World and Adventure tourism.

I am a trailing spouse. I trail around the globe setting up house and finding things to fill my time in the countries where my husband is working. Although our life sometimes looks a bit jet set to outsiders, my husband's job is far from glamorous: he is not a music producer, or documentary maker, an anthropologist or trust fund kid on an extended gap year. He is a Scottish accountant who audits banks and other financial services, and has a very sensible haircut. We have lived in Sao Paulo (first daughter), Hong Kong (second daughter), Bangkok (amazingly no experience of maternity suite!), Seoul (third daughter born) and now reside in Almaty, Kazakhstan where I am expecting our fourth (and final) baby.

I suppose we moved abroad because we wanted to try to inject some more cultural and geographical interest into our lives. We didn't see a problem with having to work things out in another language – although this was something my husband regretted when he was presented with all his working papers in Portuguese on his first day, and had to spend hours and hours translating every word with a dictionary! Once we had persuaded a company to fly us to Brazil, and pay my husband to live and work there, it all seemed like a heavenly, adventure no-brainer, and so it was.

After three years in Sao Paulo, our first daughter Beatriz arrived and that was when we started to explore with small people in tow. What a difference one tiny little person can make to a trip. I don't think it ever crossed our minds not to travel as much once we had children. We both just thought that we would do the same things, but she would come too and enjoy it as much as we did. Neither of us is totally hardcore, though, and so we didn't want our baby to be uncomfortable or unsettled by the experience, and of course we didn't want to leave her behind with grandparents or a nanny.

At the end of our time in Brazil we took a month to explore some of the destinations that were still on our wish list and joined the South American back pack circuit. This is the route which snakes mainly through

Spanish-speaking South America (how people can say they have 'done' South America if they have not visited Brazil is beyond me, but a lot of them like to think they have…) is packed with well-heeled Israeli, American and European backpackers. As well as sporting wardrobes that would look good on a night out in London, most of the flashpackers we encountered were wildly enthusiastic about the place as only adrenaline junkies can be – they rampaged around climbing volcanoes, parachuting into remote deserts, having meaningful relationships for two days on sun soaked beaches before moving onto the next stage of their itineraries. Daddy's credit card for emergencies was regularly exercised for emergency snowboard rental or airplane flights over Inca ruins – they were having an absolute blast!

Before we had kids, we would probably have done our utmost to join this merry throng. But we were no longer quite the same as this lot. For a start, we were travelling with one rucksack, a travel cot and a pushchair. Not your standard flashpacker gear! Secondly, we had to get up every day at about 5.30 am when our beloved daughter woke up. By 10.30pm most days we were happy to crawl into bed – not for us the wild bonding sessions in the local pubs getting to know our contemporaries. We had to work out ways to do the things we wanted, making the most of our trip, but not dragging little one into situations unsuitable for her delicate age. Essentially, on our first ever, proper travel abroad with Bia, we very quickly realised that contentedly, successfully and effectively travelling with children means finding a happy compromise to your child-free desires. Travelling with children does not mean that you cannot do what you might want, but you have to be imaginative and do it in a way that is going to work for all of you. And you need to have patience and a good sense of humour.

The day I finished breastfeeding Beatriz when she was eight months old, I fed her in bed, handed her over to my husband and then headed off to join a hiking group to climb Mount Villarica, a volcano in Pucon, Chile. We hiked up for four hours through snow to the summit of this spectacular, conical, live volcano. I peered into the depths of the world, with smoke, gas and the occasional bit of rock being blown out, took in the stunning view on this perfect day of the line of volcanoes stretching away along the Andres as far as the eye could see, then tobogganed down the mountainside all the way back to the mini-bus. The next day, my husband did the same climb while Beatriz and I played in town. This was the first of many situations when we changed the way we did things to accommodate childcare. But we probably remember Pucon just as much for it being the place our crawling first-born ate some dried dog poo which had fallen off a hikers boot in the dining room of our normally pristine Bed & Breakfast! Disgusting at the time, hilarious afterwards when she did not break out in spots, grow hairs on her face or start being sick.

We now have three daughters and a fourth on the way, but have never stopped exploring. We have made efforts to settle down, and have been on expensive, five star family resort holidays trying to enjoy ourselves. Of course, we do have fun (spending time together swimming, luxuriating in huge bathrooms, eating together, and being surrounded by perfectly crafted, man-made beauty – who wouldn't?) but these holiday brochure picture-perfect breaks are not for us – too boring. Ironic really, considering the marketing images of these places used to make us salivate with anticipation. We like our independence, we enjoy communicating with people and working things out even if we don't speak their language, and we want to learn something when we go away. Since our first faltering steps into the world of global travel with small people we have had some truly amazing experiences. We've ridden elephants through padi fields in Bali, climbed the Great Wall of China, visited Macchu Picchu in Peru and the Taj Mahal in India, skied in South Korea, zoomed up rivers in longtail boats through the jungles of Northern Thailand to remote hill tribe villages, camped in canyons in Kazakhstan, eaten food of unknown origin in Takayama, Japan (one of the few places where communication proved almost impossible – all we knew were the few phrases we had picked up from a Sesame Street video with Big Bird!). We never leave the kids at home and they are very excited when it is time for holidays. Along the way, we have learnt some tricks, some dos and some don'ts. Planning is key, and while you can change the details of your plan, you need to have a rough idea of where you want to be, what you want to do and how far you want to go in a certain time-frame. It is hopeless if you only start to think about what you might do that day when you are talking about it at breakfast.

I try to pack the bare minimum. In the old days, I used to take all the food and nappies we would need. But then I realised that there are babies and small children everywhere, even in the remotest places. Of course, if you are going to travel for a long time through very inhospitable territory with no shops, you need to pack some supplies – a few days of food jars, some nappies and wipes - but this is only in extreme places. Otherwise, you can make do with what is available locally, even if it is not your preferred brand. Be flexible. Breastfeeding removes a lot of hassle for travel with tiny babies, because you don't need to worry about washing bottles or carrying formula. But even when our daughter dropped her sleep-aid toy elephant down a foetid squat toilet, we were able to have it washed, boiled to sterilise it, and dried out before nightfall! People the world over, are always delighted to help out with small children if you will only ask.

You need to accept that things will happen that are not ideal: your child will be copiously sick all over you on a plane in the middle of the night after a nine-hour delay at the airport (London-Hong Kong 2003), they might wash themselves in the bucket reserved for anal cleansing in India (Delhi 2002), they may get properly ill (Thailand 2006) or be injured (Kazakhstan 2008 x 2) in which case you need to have the means to pay for a doctor or even medical evacuation. But always try to stay calm, remember that there will nearly always be a way out of a bad situation, and keep your head. Be alert. You cannot assume that things will work as you may expect when you are abroad and you need to exercise good sense. But then again, keeping a level head is quite sensible even when you are not travelling!

We have notched up many miles and a fair bit of travel experience in the last 10 years. If people ever ask me about travelling with young 'uns in tow, I have to give a qualified answer. It is not for everyone to be independent and off the beaten track. Some people just cannot manage without their home comforts. I always tell people to think about what they want to get out of an adventure trip for themselves and their children. Some people will decide to take a softer option, or perhaps an organised tour. Others, with a few useful tips buzzing around their heads, will head off with enthusiasm and have their own fantastic adventures in this amazing world.

Linda Jones

Linda Jones is mum to twins and editor of **www.havealovelytime.com**. She also blogs at **www.gotyourhandsfull.com** and when she's not pulling funny faces on rollercoasters, she is to be found at work as a director of editorial agency Passionate Media – **www.passionatemedia.co.uk**

Think holidays with a family have to be hard work? Reckon you have to put the fun you had before kids behind you? Forget it! And don't think for one second that just because you can't afford or face the prospect of packing up and heading for some far flung destination that means your sense of adventure – and most importantly fun – is doomed.

To read travel sections in newspapers and magazines, you'd think that our favourite family holidays sometimes involve exactly that – trekking to the same exotic places we did pre-children, spending an absolute fortune. You'd also think that often we don't like our children very much, preferring instead to shoehorn them in to a pretty grown up type of holiday or spend as much time as we can away from them. "How To Keep Your Kids Off Your Back This Summer," scream the headlines on travel articles and I scream a little inside. That's why I set up Have A Lovely Time. This is a site all about celebrating the good times parents and children can have together – whether that's on a beach in The Seychelles as the broadsheets would have us believe, or in a caravan park in Wales, as our wallets tell us we really should. It can be entertaining, informative and inspirational to read reports of dream destinations from those who are lucky enough to be able to afford to go, but our site recognises that the Number One consideration for most families will be price. And when people wax lyrical about a favourite holiday spot for their family, then complain about how expensive it is to get there and an arduous journey, I think it's a crying shame.

What about Pembrokeshire to marvel at the puffins on Skomer? How about seeing Mooky get up to his tricks at Blackpool circus? You could take the family to witness the beauty of a Scottish loch or accompany David Bellamy on a nature lovers' tour of a UK caravan park. Have you ever spent the day looking for castles in Cornwall or been on a family walk in the Lakes? How about laughing your head off at a talent competition laid on by Haven, Butlins or Pontins? Our writers have done those things and their children loved it. You might too! I'm not sure my children would be as mad about Bulgaria, Morocco or Sardinia, and we can't afford to risk it. And just as families can overlook what the UK has to offer, there's also a snobbery about certain types of family holiday on home shores. Mention some big names in the tourism industry and long-held prejudices will come to the fore. But if you think Butlins is all about knobbly knees, glamorous grannies and creaking chalets check again. I recently attended the launch of the £20 million Ocean spa (yes spa) hotel at Butlins Bognor Regis and it was out of this world. The activities and entertainment on offer in the rest of the park had our girls entranced from the minute we arrived.

Similarly, for us miserable Brits, Disney can make us roll our eyes and think, "It's just not for us". I know I did and I couldn't have been more wrong. When I imagined motherhood, I thought I knew where I stood. There would be no yelling at my children in shops, no sitting in front of the telly for them while I finished whatever I was doing and definitely, yes definitely, no trips to see Mickey Mouse and pals in Florida. While the first two of these rather deluded expectations were proved wrong a long way back, I resolutely stuck to the last. Every time the words, "Disney theme parks," were uttered in my house, I shrugged and looked away if I was in a good mood or muttered darkly under my breath if I was feeling a bit stressed. Over the years lots of friends have raved about Disney, about the fun to be had and the beautiful sunshine. Meanwhile, I just resigned myself to the fact that well, it wasn't for us. I was always delighted that my mates and their families had enjoyed such a lovely time but felt we couldn't afford to sample the Disney experience too. Or even if funds could stretch that far, that it was all too plastic, too false somehow, for the likes of us - more used to a holiday park in Wales or a walking break in the Lakes. But my mind was changed by a hosted trip thanks to Have A Lovely Time.

The customer service was flawless, the food a revelation and the five-star spa Swedish massage an unforgettable treat. But alongside the laughs I shared with my fellow bloggers and our unflappable Disney PR lady, my enduring memory will be of the unadulterated joy etched on kids' faces as they witnessed Cinderella, Snow White or

Mr Incredible brought to life. Now it makes me sad when other friends shrug their shoulders or turn their nose up at Disney. Why foist our adult cynicisms on our children? I bristled at the Bibbety Bobbety Bootique where little girls were made over to look like Disney princesses, thinking it was all a bit too much, too grown up. But why should my jaded grown up prejudices get in the way of the very willing models' fun? Minutes later as I saw numerous Little Mermaids clippety-clopping along with their families and beaming from ear to ear, I relaxed. Why on earth shouldn't they? I now understand why families save up to go to Florida. I never thought I would see the day! Our next stop is a Disney cruise – our about face is complete. A cruise? Whoah, that does make a change!

But for me possibly the greatest pleasure on holiday with my children is a day at the beach. To watch them squeal with joy as they try out their body boards in the crashing waves is one of life's special moments. We recently asked readers to tell us their favourite UK beaches. Pembrokeshire came out on top. I've been moved to tears by the beauty of the beaches in West Wales. Mwnt in particular is stunning, as is Llangrannog. On a hot day I bore my family rigid by announcing for the millionth time that you couldn't find better on a Greek island or the Algarve. On a windy day the sea is even better for those body boards and on a rainy day you can snuggle in a nearby café with a hot chocolate while your children tuck into waffles or one of the biggest scones you will ever see in your life.

But there are plenty more beaches to discover.

Our readers told us about the beauty and character of beaches all over our isles. From Cleethorpes to Holkham in Norfolk, and from Weymouth to the Gower Peninsular. What a pity to not see these places because our default setting is abroad. And in the spirit of celebrating what's on offer, overlooked or shunned by those who consider themselves a more discerning traveller, may I ask when was the last time you visited Blackpool? Perhaps your answer is, "Never," or perhaps it's, "No chance, not for me, thanks". Well, you guessed it, I have plenty to say about said much-maligned seaside town and it's all because of the fun my family have had there. Maybe you've never considered going to Blackpool because of its bad press. But, let me assure you, as with Butlins and Disney, preconceptions are there to be smashed. I don't know how many times I have been to Blackpool, but it's quite a few. My daughters are 10, and they have had three weekends there already, plus a day trip to the Pleasure Beach in the rain last year for their birthday. Why did Tigger have his head down the toilet? He was looking for Pooh. This is not the best joke in the world, granted. But when you are six, it is pretty good. And it's the sort of joke to be heard uttered by Mooky the clown at Blackpool Circus. We love, love, love Mooky. We laughed until we could laugh no more at him the first time we went to see the circus and the second. Absolutely brilliant. A couple of years back ringmaster Harvey Seager read out birthday greetings for our daughters and their cousins - even though one of them wasn't for another six months. Priceless. The whole spectacle is quite a show with lots of excitement and sharp intakes of breath from the audience at the feats on display. This is a marvellous celebration of variety and talent from all around the world and has been going much longer than Simon Cowell.

The Tower itself is beautiful, though it's expensive to get in. We like to sit and watch the world go by, marvelling at the couples in their finery as they take to the floor, enjoy a cream tea or listen to the organist. And what about the Illuminations? I think I first went when I was about four. Three generations of my family made the trip and my dad has the hotel key ring photos to prove it. If you've heard Blackpool called the Vegas of the North, then this is why! The six miles or so of lights are said to attract more than three million people a year. I hope they all like chips.

So there you have it – a quick amble from me around some of the holiday hotspots you may have ignored or spurned. Why not give them a go? What have you got to lose except possibly your temper when you chew on an Economy sausage? You have everything to gain. See these places and holidays from a children's eye view. You'll be glad you did, I promise you.

Tips and Advice...
Easy To Navigate Advice

This book was never meant to be just a practical guide but tales of our experiences travelling as a family, both short and long-term, with a healthy dose of tips running throughout. I hope you have enjoyed our story and the places we have visited and that our ability to travel with our daughter might inspire you to travel in a way that suits your lifestyle. To help you plan your own adventures I have collated here all the advice I have inserted at certain times throughout the book (as well as a few extras) and I hope they will be easy to refer to and useful.

B&Bs and Self Catering

Always find out how child-friendly accommodation is. Consider things such as do they have a cot, is there a secure garden, can you get a buggy to the accommodation.

Bathing

We have bathed Isabella in many sinks on campsites and in various accommodations. While children are small enough, this is an ideal solution in the absence of a bath.

If no bath or sink is available we found that by taking her in the shower and holding her close, we could give her a good wash, but sadly not without a few tears!

Beach

A Factor 50 beach tent is a great idea. A pop up one is small enough to fit in your luggage and perfect if your baby wants a rest on the beach. They can get quite warm inside so try to pitch them in the shade.

Little Swimmer nappies or waterproof swimming knickers are perfect for small babies who can splash around to their heart's content without you worrying about them leaving a present for fellow bathers! We also found that the nappies can in fact be dried and reused… if they are clean of course!

We always try to get out first thing in the morning to the beach. By the time it starts to get really hot you want to be safely in the shade of your balcony enjoying a beer while your baby takes an afternoon nap.

Camping & Caravanning

We would have loved to travel in a VW camper, but with a baby and a dog, this would not have been practical. If you're planning on doing a similar trip short or long-term, do consider how much space you need to move around, change your baby's bum, as well as have a little of your own space when baby goes to bed.

The thing about small babies and children is that if you get them used to things young, you stand a good chance of them being quite amenable when it comes to fitting in with things. Because Isabella was in a routine she got used to sleeping in her own curtained area of the camper with neither party causing much disturbance for the other. I'm not sure I would want to do this long-term after the age of two, but with a baby it was fine.

A top-notch campsite really does have something for all the family and none are better than those in France. So whether you are just planning a camping getaway, or you too are venturing on the road long-term, I would highly recommend indulging in a bit of camping luxury for the first few nights.

When your baby insists on keeping fellow campers up all night the best way to deal with the fallout is to face it head-on. Smile and apologise and you'll find most will be understanding. Who knows what they're saying when they turn away. But who cares?!

Although at the beginning of our long-term travels we chose to stay on campsites, over time we have realised how easily you can stay in places for free.

Designated picnic areas can be found throughout Europe, usually with water and loos. Obviously, if you have a camper/caravan with a toilet/shower inside you will be able to rough it quite comfortably for longer!

The hardest thing for us as a family on the road was when the rain came as it hampered so many things and made life much harder. The only way to stay upbeat was to think of creative things to do like making giant bouncy castles out of all the cushions or having a musical afternoon using every pot, pan, bowl and wooden spoon we could find. You might want to take a few board games with you if you have older children.

Car

When you're heading off on a long car journey make sure you have a good selection of stories and children's nursery rhymes on CD. They can be a godsend when nothing else will do and mesmerised my daughter.

Always carry a few emergency toys in the car; toys your baby doesn't get to see or play with very often. Try adult items you're not worried about, such as a glovebox map, or pick up a few of the plentiful toys on offer in newsagents and whip them out at difficult moments. There's nothing like something new to recapture interest and the result is a content baby leaving mummy and daddy to peacefully enjoy the scenery outside the window.

One thing we did find is that journeys in the heat were a serious no no with a baby and dog in the car. We had to leave early in the morning or travel through the night to avoid misery and remember to carry plenty of water.

If you are thinking of a long road trip, do it when your baby is young. Although off-putting to some, young babies are transportable and adaptable. Equals: few (I didn't say no) tantrums and grumps at being cooped up in the car for hours at a time.

Changing & Toileting

A backpack is more practical as a nappy bag than a shoulder bag.

Although I have since become a pro at one-handed nappy changing, I still maintain that teamwork is best. If you do not have an extra pair of hands ensure everything you will need is laid out on the seat ready to go. You don't want to be rooting through a bag on the floor for wipes with one hand whilst trying to ensure your baby doesn't roll of the seat with the other, in order to deal with unexpected projectile pee!

Babies exist the world over. You really don't need to pack your suitcase with hundreds of nappies; just pick up a pack at a local chemist.

Some changing facilities are basic, to say the least. Please, please, please make sure you pack a portable changing mat.

When you're travelling with a baby there really is no room for being shy. If your baby needs a bum change and there is no discreet place for this to happen, you must be brash and take care of things in the most comfortable place you can. I can't deny that I tend to send Scott to do the really brash bum-changing duties.

On the road and in many new locations we still had various obstacles to overcome. Potty training is one example and so when we picked olives her potty came with us to the field!

City Breaks

Consider self-catering accommodation in a city as it provides a home-from-home environment for you and your baby and means that you can work out your own itinerary which for us, with a young baby in a demanding routine, was imperative.

Although we were lucky to stumble on a quiet Athens during Easter week, it would be wise when visiting a city with a little one to think about when it is likely to be a little quieter. I think it is less overwhelming for little eyes and ears and ensures a happier and more relaxed experience all round.

When visiting a city choose lots of activities to keep your baby happy. We allowed Isabella to run free in parks in between doing the things we wanted to do and we found that small, relaxed cafes were a much better option than trying to sit down to a fancy lunch in a posh restaurant.

We have found that it is still possible to visit cities with a small baby and a dog; you simply have to be more aware of what you can and can't do. Museums, theatre and restaurants were a no-no for us, but walking through the cobbled streets enjoying lunch al-fresco and Nutella crepes was satisfactory for all the family.

Try not to drive through or round busy cities in the heat of the day with a baby on board. They will probably be fine, but you will be at risk of injecting unnecessary tension into your relationship!

Confidence & Consideration

You must develop a thick skin when people are negative about your plans to travel with a young baby. Have a handy stock of phrases to hand. I particularly like to throw in the fact that my parents took a road trip right round Scandinavia with three young children in the Sixties... and survived to tell the very interesting tale. This usually shuts people up!

Get as much travel as you can in with a newborn; they get used to it fast, as do you, and you'll learn quickly from your mistakes. Plus, it's often much easier with a baby than it is with a two-year-old. Trust me!

If you're not sure whether independent travel is for you then consider whether you would have gone for such options before becoming parents. The odds are that if you were not up for the challenge when single, you most certainly won't be with your child on board!

When it comes to long-term options, travelling before your child reaches school age is an excellent idea. If you have notions of open-ended travel and are able to give up work altogether or take a sabbatical, start packing now!

If you intend to travel long-term with a young baby you might be as well to wait until they are about a year old, when they will have had their main and most important jabs.

Feeding

If you are in the car take hot water in a flask to warm bottles on the go; although many babies are completely used to milk at room temperature, I think a warm bottle is comforting first and last thing.

In our experience, most restaurants and bars in Mediterranean countries are happy to provide a bowl of hot water for your baby's bottle– don't be afraid to ask!

Always pack a few ready-made milk cartons if you're not breast-feeding. They are perfect if you're caught out unawares.

To save on packing do try local formula milk from the chemist. It's nothing to be scared of and you will often recognise International brands. Never fear – there will always be someone who can help you out and failing that, carry a good dictionary!

A rucksack with a cool compartment for made-up bottles is handy if you're heading out for long walks.

Sterilise bottles in any sink or bowl; just don't forget your sterilising tablets.

Isabella joins us at all restaurant meals. In the absence of a high chair, a chair with arms and strategically placed cushions works a treat - in a French restaurant the owner even brought her childhood wooden highchair out!

Expect the proprietor to take your baby on a restaurant tour while you eat; this happens a lot in Europe.

Once Isabella was on to solids we tried her with everything. At 15 months she loved curry, olives, stuffed vine leaves and tapas.

Hotels

If you stay in a city, choose a central hotel so you can get to all the sites easily with your baby.

Don't forget to check that your room is baby-safe i.e.: no unsecure balconies, and whether they have a cot available.

Out On The Town

We often travel with a baby carrier but when you're planning lots of late nights in tavernas, a buggy doubles up as a bed.

I believe wholeheartedly that introducing your child to late night Fiestas and Fetes can never be a bad thing. Isabella's eyes lit up as we pushed her around such events and we felt she was getting a wonderful experience of different cultures.

Throughout Europe most bars and restaurants were child-friendly and not many batted an eyelid at Isabella's presence. The best countries were Spain and Greece.

Packing

Write a list and then cull. You never need as much as you think and a carefully-packed bag gives the illusion of having less than you do while making you a modern Mary Poppins!

Most babies will go through two outfits each day. If you're going somewhere hot for a week, take seven outfits and wash each one daily in the shower. Hey presto, 14 outfits to cover all eventualities.

Forget suitcases. A large backpack is much easier to handle.

Always carry a basic First Aid kit to include Calpol, insect repellent, plasters, antiseptic cream and sun lotion.

When you are travelling somewhere cold, take an all-in-one all weather suit. You will never regret this.

When you're heading off on a varied trip with lots of different modes of transport, travel light when it comes to clothes. For Isabella we would pack a small selection of outfits, a Kagool, several sleepsuits and then we layered her in a really warm outfit for the plane. Always work out how many outfits you can hand-wash and get dry.

I say it again and again - there is no need to take huge numbers of large toys if you're heading off on a long-term road trip. There is usually something much more interesting going on and you will just find yourself lugging them about for no reason. We dragged around a huge fold out farm on a recent road trip because 'she loved it'... but not when travelling it seems!

Tips For Peace And Quiet

Little boxes of sultanas are healthy and picking them out of the box keeps babies content for quite some time.

When babies are past the newborn stage they must have plenty to keep them occupied if you expect them to stay cheerful while you're knocking back cappuccinos and chatting to friends. A little rucksack containing books, a pull-along toy and various other bits and bobs works a treat, for a while anyway.

Toys Isabella is familiar with will not hold her attention if she feels irritable. I therefore always have a handful of new items or toys that she has never seen before, or that she sees as forbidden. Whip these out when the pressure gets too much.

Plane

The biggest misconception ever is that short-haul plane travel with a newborn is difficult. When they are very small it is about as easy as it gets. They will normally sleep peacefully in your arms whilst joyously lapping up milk as and when needed, in particular at fractious moments. When they are a bit older you'll be wrestling with a boisterous child who requires constant stimulation, whether they are used to travel or not!

Getting an extra seat for your baby is really a bonus that is worth some extra work! The extra space is a godsend when it comes to manoeuvrability for all.

Air Hostesses are more than happy to let your baby toddle along the gangway… they love to coo!

Note that fellow passengers are 'mostly' a lot more understanding when you are on a flight to a holiday destination. You might get a few glaring, but you're normally pretty safe from single businessmen who hate travelling near tots.

Do your best to book a flight around nap or evening sleep time. There is nothing better than giving your baby a bottle at take-off and watching them slip into a slumber for the rest of the flight. Make sure you go to the loo first though - you won't want to disturb them!

Preparation & Planning

Pay extra for the Post Office to check through your passport application before sending to the passport office. It saves them sending it back and delaying proceedings.

Babies are NOT expected to have their eyes open for passport photos!

Make sure you carefully consider your own needs when planning a trip. What might have been a simple nighttime adventure when you were single could leave you looking like an extra from Thriller with a baby in tow.

We decided to wait until Isabella was a year old before heading off on a long adventure. She had had most of her early immunisations and we had managed to get a few trips in to check that we were all up for it on a longer-term basis.

I wish I could give you a top tip about the best time to leave behind your life to enter into open-ended travel, but I can't. There really is no good time to take such a big jump – you simply have to remind yourself of the dreams you have and work towards them.

The one thing you need to worry least about, though, is your child. If they are young, they will surprise you with their acceptance of new routines and new surroundings. Of course, if you are in a position to rent your property out to go travelling then this would be ideal.

Not only will learning at least some of a language be useful in sticky situations, you will find that as it is likely your baby will be mixing with local children, knowing enough to make small talk with their parents will come in very handy.

For me, the hugest benefit of longer-term travel when your child is small is the time you are able to spend together as a family. School and independence comes far too quickly and our travelling life in Isabella's early years, I hope, will create a lasting bond.

Sleeping

The single best investment you can make if you want your baby to be super transportable is a Samsonite pop up bubble cot. We have used ours for numerous dinner parties and taken it with us on holidays (it will fit in your luggage or can be taken as hand luggage) and for the little one, it has been a home from home.

In the absence of a cot, we have made many a bed out of quilts and pillows where Isabella has been more than happy!

A traditional travel cot is a must when you're on the road, certainly up to the age of 18 months. Not only is it the perfect sleeping place (we had ours on top of the camper bed!) but when you are busy putting up your tent or setting out your camper, you will be glad of somewhere to put your baby safely.

You will be surprised at how adaptable babies are and also at their ability to sleep amidst unbelievable noise.

Travelling (while you are there)

When your child looks at something, no matter how simple, look at it with them. Hold still your usual dismissive judgment that it is probably something boring and dig deep. Trust me when I say that it's a revelation to find yourself utterly absorbed with the antics of an ant!

Make snow angels. Go on woodland walks to the unknown. Be reckless; think less. You might be surprised at what you find!

Travelling in Mediterranean countries with a baby is really quite something. You will quickly get used to walking into any shop, from the bakery to the supermarket, and being given free gifts for your little one. And when people reach out to take your baby, don't worry, it is perfectly normal for this to happen so my advice is to sit back and enjoy a beer!

I am often asked how we adapted to travelling life as a family and how we could enjoy things with a demanding baby on our back. I have to say that I wholeheartedly believe that if you embrace your child into your life, they will become comfortable with all that you do. We are surprised at how adaptable Isabella is within our lifestyle. Don't be afraid to step out of your holiday comfort zone... you might be surprised at what you will find!

If you plan to spend a few months in a different country to that of your own you will need to consider carefully what this might mean for your young child/children. If you don't know anyone you might feel daunted but I can assure you there is always a park or a nursery in a nearby town where you can go, armed with a dictionary. If your child is very small you might also think about hooking up with fellow ex-pat mums in the area. Although the idea of only mixing with locals is romantic and authentic, as a young mother in a strange land I have found it is equally important to have a few friends who share your language.

Spanish & Greek bars and restaurants are different. Yes they are family orientated, but people can and do smoke happily around children. This would upset many people, especially those of us aware of the danger this puts on small children, but we made the decision that certain things within moderation were to be accepted during our travelling adventure and you need to be aware and consider these factors before you head inside.

Useful Items

Slings are a great option for travel when you're baby is small. Attempting to fold and unfold your buggy whilst simultaneously trying to remove or strap in your baby and hail a taxi is a nightmare. Strap your baby to you as soon as you exit the plane and keep them there – it will also give you peace of mind when it comes to taxi rides.

We use a Mountain Buggy when we travel. It's essential for many terrains, doubles-up as a sleeping place and we can strap the bubble cot to it in transit, thus getting away with loading them both into the hold! (Normally you are limited to one cot or one buggy.) I think that if we could recommend one buggy from birth to when they leave it behind, a mountain buggy is it.

One of the best items we took away with us in our camper was the Bumbo – a kind of little seat that sits quite steadily on most surfaces and keeps baby in a good sitting position. When my oldest and dearest friend gave it to us as a present I didn't really understand it, but it has proved invaluable in so many situations.

Walking

When our daughter was born we were lucky enough to be passed down some wonderful items, one of which was a backpack. The backpack became indispensable from about the age of 8 months and can be used up to the age of 3. It's perfect if you are into walking or navigating your way through the cobbled and steep alleyways of traditional French towns!

Working Holidays

HELPX.net is a great place to find volunteer opportunities on farms all over the world. There is often the opportunity to negotiate terms (usually board and food in return for work) to allow for the whole family to take part.

Useful Websites

- www.babyworld.co.uk
- www.totstotravel.co.uk
- www.travelblogs.com
- www.twittermoms.com
- www.britishmummybloggers.ning.com
- www.jojomamanbebe.co.uk
- www.kidsoup.tv
- www.glossa-houses.com
- www.alanrogers.com
- www.campingcheque.co.uk
- www.helpx.net
- www.mumsensemagazine.com
- www.sunnews.es

Bibliography

The Rough Guide to Spain, Various Authors, ISBN-10: 1843537605, ISBN-13: 978-1843537601

The Rough Guide to France, Various Authors, ISBN-10: 1848360290, ISBN-13: 978-1848360297

The Rough Guide to Norway, Phil Lee, ISBN-10: 1848360274, ISBN-13: 978-1848360273

The Rough Guide to Greek Islands, Various Authors, ISBN-10: 1858289483, ISBN-13: 978-1858289489

Walking in France (Lonely Planet Walking Guide), various authors, ISBN-10: 1740592433, ISBN-13: 978-1740592437

Alan Rogers Europe 2009: Quality Camping and Caravanning Sites, ISBN-10: 1906215146, ISBN-13: 978-1906215149

As I Walked Out One Midsummer Morning, Laurie Lee, ISBN-10: 0140033181, ISBN-13: 978-0140033182

Driving Over Lemons: An Optimist in Andalucía, Chris Stewart, ISBN-10: 0953522709, ISBN-13: 978-0953522705

The Alchemist: A Fable About Following Your Dream, Paulo Coelho, ISBN-10: 0722532938, ISBN-13: 978-0722532935

The Virgin Blue, Tracy Chevalier, ISBN-10: 0007241461, ISBN-13: 978-0007241460

Prodigal Summer, Barbara Kingsolver, ISBN-10: 0571206484, ISBN-13: 978-0571206483

Auto da Fay, Fay Weldon, ISBN-10: 000710992X, ISBN-13: 978-0007109920

About Alice Griffin

Alice Griffin's hunger for adventure started at a young age and was fuelled by her parent's love of unorthodox travel and evenings spent with the family atlas being tested on names of countries and cities around the globe. She was keen to move  on from imaginary trips and at age 23 her dreams came true when she embarked on a six-month stint in Japan. Instead of satisfying her desires this experience simply fired her passion, and she has spent the ten years since exploring the world, both as a tourist and as a travel writer for a UK-based tourist guide.

Eventually love and marriage came along and when pregnant with her first child Alice began to wonder if the rumours were true: that her days of independent travel were now over. As she pondered the idea of a life without the exciting and spontaneous travel she had always enjoyed, she quickly realised that this was not entirely suited to her normally free-spirited self and decided to keep travelling anyway, with daughter Isabella firmly strapped to her chest.

Alice has written travel articles and appeared in various publications both online and in print including: Babyworld, Spain magazine, Real Travel, Living Abroad and Dogs Today. In addition she writes a family travel column for US-based website, Twittermoms, the Women Zone column for the Spanish Sun newspaper and the Travel Sense section for Mumsense, a new family lifestyle magazine. She loves to share with others her passion for the world and in particular, show fellow parents that travel with a baby need not be as daunting or as stressful as some might think!

Seven Things You Never Knew About Alice

1. Alice is a vegetarian and no, she doesn't eat fish...

2. Her favourite meal is toad in the hole made by her dad (with veggie sausages of course!)

3. Alice loves puddings, and treacle tart and custard made by her mum is a favourite (mum's puddings have even made their way through the post to Japan!)

4. When not on travels Alice likes nothing better than curling up on the sofa with a good film, her husband... and her knitting.

5. She is actually quite shy in person, but you maybe wouldn't think it.

6. Alice dreams of owning a small crumbling cottage with spectacular views and a horse at the end of the garden.

7. She left school at 16 to train as a secretary and knows only too well what it feels like to spend many, many hours staring out of office windows dreaming of escape. She reminds herself of these times when trying to live a life less ordinary proves challenging.

Hire Alice

Freelance Writer, Traveller, Author, Columnist

Since the age of three Alice has been writing words in dog-eared notebooks, but she has made a living out of her passion for the past ten years. From personal scribbles she moved on to local publications before landing her dream job travelling the world writing for a tourist guide. This experience saw her end up in a number of crazy but exhilarating situations, such as driving the amazing ice-fields parkway in Alberta, Canada on the day they shut the road due to snowstorms, being deposited onto the most rudimentary of taxis somewhere in the middle of nowhere outside Chang Mai, Thailand and flying over the amazing

Arizona landscapes in an ever-so-slightly scary plane. When Alice returned from globetrotting she studied journalism in London and now writes freelance articles in the areas of travel and women's interest.

Her passion for living out of a backpack remains and along with her husband, young daughter and dog she has just returned from a long-term family road trip through France, Spain and Portugal. Parts of this journey are included in her first book ~ Tales from a Travelling Mum ~ and plans for an Eastern Europe & Scandinavia road trip are taking shape for 2010.

Aside from travelling, writing freelance articles and books, Alice also pens the Women Zone column for the Spanish Sun newspaper, a family life column for US-based website, Twittermoms, and she writes the Travel Sense section for Mumsense magazine.

For stories and articles contact Alice directly:

Telephone: +44 7879 213 813
Email: alice@alicegriffin.co.uk
Website: www.alicegriffin.co.uk